The Hawaiian Islands

Second Edition

Doug Wallin

51195

9 781559 920384

Pisces Books
A division of Gulf Publishing Company
Houston, Texas

Publisher's note: At the time of publication of this book, all the information was determined to be as accurate as possible. However, new construction may have changed land reference points, weather may have altered reef configurations, and some businesses may no longer be in operation. Your assistance in keeping future editions up-to-date will be greatly appreciated.

Also, please pay particular attention to the diver rating system in this book. Know your limits!

All photographs by Doug Wallin, except where noted.

Library of Congress Cataloging-in-Publication Data

Wallin, Doug.
    Diving and snorkeling guide to the Hawaiian Islands / Doug Wallin. — 2nd ed.
        p.   cm.
    Includes index.
    ISBN 1-55992-038-6
    1. Skin diving—Hawaii—Guide-books. 2. Scuba diving—Hawaii—Guide-books. 3. Hawaii—Description and travel—1981—Guide-books. I. Title.
GV840.S78W28   1991
797.2'3—dc20   90-25680
                                                                CIP

Printed in Hong Kong

10 9 8 7 6 5 4 3 2 1

Contents

In the deeper area of the Blowhole, a ledge drops from 20–60 feet (6–18 meters), framing a diver against the bright, tropical sun.

How to Use This Guide

This book provides information that both residents and visitors to Hawaii can use when evaluating snorkeling and scuba locations on the four major Hawaiian islands: Oahu, Maui, the Big Island, and Kauai. Dive sites on the nearby islet of Molokini and some more accessible sites on the island of Lanai are usually included when mentioning Maui; however, because of its relative isolation, no sites on Molokini are included because of their inaccessibility to the average diver. Descriptions for each dive site include typical water conditions, depth ranges, recommended entries and exits (including maps), what you can expect to see in the way of topography and marine life, the skill level needed, and more.

For newcomers to Hawaii, and even for experienced divers, it is strongly recommended that initial snorkel and scuba excursions be made with a dive shop or dive-tour company. Dive sites from one area of an island to another can vary greatly in diveability due to the differing wind, water, current, and weather conditions that can exist around an island at any given time. During the winter months, for instance, diving can be treacherous on the north shore of any island because of heavy ocean swells and surf, while, at the same time, the leeward (wind sheltered) areas may offer calm waters and beautiful diving conditions.

If you decide to go snorkeling or scuba diving on your own rather than with an organized tour, be sure to study your intended dive site carefully. Consult a local dive shop in the area to check recent weather and water conditions. If the site you have chosen hasn't been good lately, most shops can suggest a better one and save you the wasted time of going to an unfavorable and possibly hazardous location. As a general rule, diving weather and water conditions are best from about March to September. June, July, and August are especially good, as they are the best of the balmy summer months. Winter offers colder waters and a greater chance of rain and offshore storms, which can ruin diving island-wide for days at a time.

The Rating System for Divers and Dives

Novice is considered to be someone in decent physical condition who has recently completed a basic certification diving course, or a certified diver who has not been diving recently or who has no experience in similar waters. Consider *intermediate* to be a certified diver in excellent

1

physical condition who has been diving recently in similar waters. An *advanced* diver is someone who has completed an advanced certification diving course, has been diving recently in similar waters, and is in excellent physical condition. You will have to decide if you are capable of making any particular dive, depending on your level of training, recency of experience, and physical condition, as well as water conditions at the site. Remember that water conditions can change at any time, even during a dive!

The recommended diving sites in Hawaii are presented in four chapters, one for each major island group. Locations have been chosen to provide the full gamut of underwater experience, from easily accessible shallow-water reefs teeming with tropical fish, to cave diving, wreck diving, and night diving. Sites have also been chosen to include both snorkeling and scuba diving locations that can satisfy everyone from the novice skin diver to the long-time scuba enthusiast.

Hawaii's sky-blue waters promise much and deliver more to the scuba diver and snorkeler. All types of watersports are the favored recreation at Waikiki Beach.

1

Overview of the Hawaiian Islands

The Hawaiian Islands represent the northernmost extent of Polynesia, which means "many islands." The area is also referred to as the Polynesian Triangle, which extends from New Zealand, northeast to Hawaii, and southeast to Easter Island. Hawaii itself is the most isolated archipelago in the world, lying more than 2,000 miles (3,200 kilometers) from the nearest major land mass. This, along with the fact that these islands are contained in 6,500 square miles (16,640 square kilometers) of water, explains why Hawaii was one of the last major island chains in the Pacific to be populated.

The Early Polynesians. The origin of the Polynesians, of whom Hawaiians are a part, is even today somewhat questionable, and research is still ongoing. Much of the difficulty in determining their origin stems from the fact that the Polynesians never developed a written language. As a result, their history was recorded through a system of elaborate narrative chants. It is very difficult to put events in chronological order using only the information recorded in such chants, where time is measured by generations and the length of reigns of chiefs instead of years. It was not until 1821, when American missionaries first arrived in the islands, that a Hawaiian alphabet and written language were developed. A great effort was then made by the missionaries to write down as much historical knowledge as could be learned from the islanders.

Polynesians are imaginative people, and tales of gods, demons, and supernatural events permeate their lore. Thus, it is often hard to separate fact from fiction.

It has not been until recently, in fact, that modern scientific methods have evolved to help study the past. Disciplines such as linguistics, carbon dating, archaeology, and anthropology have greatly aided the determination of the history of the Polynesians. Today, this story is fairly complete and accurate, encompassing events from the birth of the Polynesian race to the present.

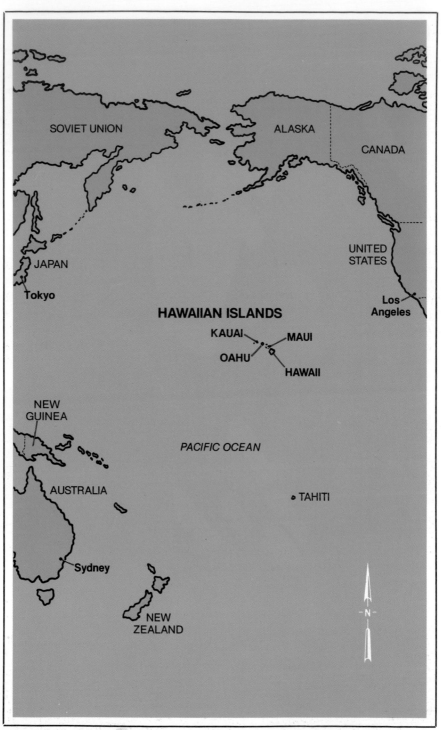

Isolated by more than 2,000 miles of ocean, the Hawaiian Islands went undiscovered for more than 250 years after the Europeans first began exploring the Pacific.

Oahu

Oahu is the main island in the Hawaiian chain; the name means "the gathering place," which is appropriate because Honolulu is the state capital and Oahu holds most of Hawaii's more than one million residents. Honolulu has blossomed into one of the major business crossroads of the world. Tourism is undeniably the state's leading industry, with more than 5 million visitors winging their way in and out each year — more than 5 times the entire resident population coming and going every 12 months. Oahu is also home to Waikiki's glittering "miracle mile."

As the population center of the state, Oahu is the most developed island industrially — and that includes the tourist industry. The great majority of hotels and condominiums are located in or very near Waikiki and its strands of golden sand beaches. Within the Waikiki/Honolulu area you will find a vast array of souvenir and gift shops, famous restaurants seving international cuisine, movie theaters, stage shows and night clubs, luaus, and much more. There is also the Ala Moana Shopping Center, one of the largest shopping complexes in the world. All Oahu is serviced by a good bus system and a plethora of tour companies, so a rental car is by no means mandatory. There are numerous dive shops around Oahu, as well as dozens of dive tour and diving equipment rental companies to handle your diving needs.

Hawaii was settled by Polynesians, who arrived in the 8th century A.D. aboard voyaging canoes like this replica, built by the Polynesian Voyaging Society.

An actor in the Kodak Hula Show portraying King Kamehameha the Great wears a cape similar to those worn by early Hawaiian rulers. Such capes were made from the feathers of as many as 80,000 birds.

Sightseeing. A hike through the lush green rain forest of Manoa Valley is highly recommended. Literally translated, the name means Rainbow Valley, and it is a popular local spot. The valley is the one right behind Honolulu. Follow the signs into Manoa and you'll find Paradise Park, another great spot to explore. The road narrows beyond the park, soon becoming a dirt road ending in a trail. This trail winds for about 1 mile (1½ kilometers) through Manoa's primordial rain forest, ending at the headwaters of a spectacular double waterfall.

For something really different, try the glider plane rides at Mokuleia, on Oahu's north shore.

Two other places hold particular interest for those who like the ocean and the creatures that inhabit it: at the far east end of Waikiki, just below Diamond Head, is the Waikiki Aquarium; on the far eastern edge of the Oahu coast is Makapuu Point, home of Sea Life Park.

For a time-machine ride back into Hawaiian and Polynesian history and culture, the Polynesian Cultural Center in Laie is a must.

Great Restaurants. Gastronomically speaking, Oahu is a glutton's delight. Within a very small area, restaurants featuring menus from all over the world can be found. For elegant (and expensive) dining, try the French restaurant, Chez Michelle, or John Dominis overlooking the ocean in Honolulu. Economical but excellent food is found at Ray's Seafood in the Waikiki Shopping Plaza. A popular family coffee shop in Waikiki is King's Bakery. For the best in Chinese fare, quite reasonably priced, visit McCully Chop Suey on the corner of McCully and King streets. If you journey to the north shore, two highly recommended places are the Crouching Lion on the windward side, and the Proud Peacock restaurant in Waimea Falls Park.

Maui

Following close on Oahu's heels, Maui is the second most popular island to visit in Hawaii. In fact, returning visitors often bypass Honolulu altogether and make straight for Maui. For many residents and visitors alike, Maui is "no ka oi" (the best).

Maui is divided geographically and geologically into two lobes, actually two volcanic mountain tops, which merge into East and West Maui. The action on the island is located on the leeward shores, the three main centers being Kihei/Wailea on East Maui, and Lahaina and Kaanapali on West Maui.

Second only to Waikiki as a tourist mecca, Kaanapali Beach and Resort Complex is located west of Lahaina and stretches for several miles around the western perimeter of the island to the luxury resort area of Kapalua. Kihei, a 45-minute drive from Lahaina to the east, is also a developed resort area but on a scale less frenetic than Kaanapali. If you like to be

The coasts of the islands are littered with small volcanic islets like Oahu's Rabbit Islands. Often, the reefs near them are honeycombed with lava-tube caverns.

in the thick of things, enjoy fine cuisine in elegant surroundings, and in general, keep one hand on the pulse of civilization, Kaanapali is the place to stay. If, on the other hand, you wish the amenities of the modern world tempered with a more relaxed, even country-like atmosphere, Kihei should be your base of operations.

Sightseeing. One of the unique abovewater attractions of Maui is historic Lahaina town. Lahaina was the capital of Hawaii long before Honolulu. In the mid-19th century it was the hub of the once great Pacific whaling industry, a seaport town where rowdy sea-roughened sailors caroused along narrow streets, with missionaries frequently throwing them in jail whenever they became too unruly. Today Lahaina is a place where the past lives into the present: a hundred years back into Hawaiian history with all the comforts of the modern world.

Hotels and Restaurants. Maui's natural creations are free to enjoy, but not so those built by man. Be prepared for Maui: it is not cheap! From Kaanapali to Kapalua, hotels and condos are expensive; Kihei and Wailea somewhat less so. If you wish for economy, the historic Pioneer Inn in Lahaina is small, informal, clean, and relatively inexpensive. If you wish to stay in Kaanapali itself, but still with an eye on economy, the Kaanapali Beach Hotel is one of the better bargains on the beach. For a very nice condo (and quite reasonably priced!), check out the Coconut Plantation in Napili.

As in most places, the cost of hotel food tends to be high. For breakfast, lunch, and dinner, oddly named Moose McGillicudy's on Front Street in Lahaina serves delicious, imaginative meals at reasonable prices. The Rusty Harpoon on Kaanapali Beach has excellent barbecue-your-own dinners, prices moderate. Casual La Familia Mexican Restaurant in Kihei and Tortilla Flats in Lahaina can't be beat for all-around prices and food quality. For more elegant yet affordable dining, Kapalua Grill and Bar offers spectacular ocean scenery and fine cuisine. And don't miss the Hyatt Hotel's bar, which can be entered by an underground swimming pool!

◀ *Construction in historic Lahaina town reflects the bygone 19th-century whaling era.*

The Big Island of Hawaii

Aptly named, the Big Island is the largest island in the Hawaiian chain. Also named Hawaii, the Big Island was so named to distinguish it from the other islands in the chain. Without a doubt, the Big Island offers the most varied abovewater scenery in the state. If you come during the winter months, you can spend the morning on the warm tropical beaches, then in the afternoon drive up the volcanic mountain of Mauna Kea and do some snow skiing!

Hilo. Hilo is not the visitor destination Kona is, nor is it intended to be. Hilo is much more rural and residential. On the windward side of the island, Hilo gets the brunt of the tradewinds all year — the idyllic calm South Seas beaches characteristic of the leeward side are missing. However, it is a gorgeous area to visit, and there are some very nice hotels and restaurants at some of the best prices in the state.

Hilo's Liluiokalani Gardens Park is a botanical and landscape extravaganza. A recommended hotel is the decidedly scenic Sheraton Waiakea Village with its rooms, restaurants, lounges, and shopping arcade built around tropical pools and palm-fringed ponds. For all-you-can-eat-and-drink Sunday champagne brunch, don't miss the Naniloa Surf Hotel.

Hawaii Volcano National Park. If you have a day or two extra to spend (not including diving), visit the volcanoes.

Perched on the slopes of the world's largest active volcano, Mauna Loa, is a natural phenomenon—Kilauea crater. Kilauea has been active for many years now, and shows little sign of letting up its volcanic outpouring to the sea.

Volcano House is a quaint, informal hotel built on the very edge of Kilauea crater (though safely many miles away from the volcanic activity!). A helicopter ride over the actual eruption site is a never-to-be-forgotten experience.

Kona. Kona is where the main thrust of the Big Island's visitor industry is located. This island is not known for its beaches: there are some nice ones, but they are few. Most of the Big Island diving is done by boat. If you stay in Kona proper, a very nice hotel with its own beach is the King Kamehameha. A modest number of dive shops and underwater tour-boat companies are located within a few blocks. South of Kona is the Keahou Bay area, featuring some nice hotels and condos, with several dive tour-boat companies to serve you. Stretching up the volcanic rocky coastline north of Kona to Puako are a number of isolated hotels and resorts where you can really get away from it all. Spots such as the Kona Village Resort, Sheraton Royal Waikaloa, and the fabulous Mauna Kea Beach Hotel are built on gorgeous beaches and offer terrific diving that can be set up through the hotel activity desks.

Kauai

Known as the "Garden Isle," Kauai is the island where people go to get away from it all. Lushly green Kauai is considered by many to be the most beautiful island in the Hawaiian chain.

Visitors arrive at the quiet little airport in residential Lihue, as there are no visitor facilities here per se. From Lihue, arrivals move to Poipu to the south or Kapaa and Hanalei to the north.

Kapaa is a residential town where some very nice, reasonably priced hotels and the Coconut Plantation shopping village have been built to entertain visitors. The beaches are nice but don't offer much in the way of diving, which can be found more on the south and north shore areas.

Sightseeing. The real visitor meccas on Kauai are found on the north shore of Hanalei/Princeville and the south shore of Poipu.

The north shore, of course, catches more weather. It does have some excellent diving sites but, due to the sometimes quickly varying moods of wind and water, it is best to go with a dive tour to dive safely. The island's best, easiest, nearly year-round dive sites are found on the leeward southern shore. The beaches of Poipu are gorgeous and you will find the greatest variety of hotel and condo accommodations, as well as a plethora of dive shops and skin and scuba tour and equipment rental outfits. Abovewater, Kauai offers a truly varied range of activities and sightseeing. It is an excellent place for visitors who have a mixture of divers and non-divers in their group. While the old salts are down under, there will always be something to keep the landlubbers busy and occupied.

Although the entire state of Hawaii is surrounded by open ocean water, on the near shore reefs shark sightings are infrequent. Hammerhead sharks, in fact, such as this small one, are a rarity to see on a dive.

2

Diving in the Hawaiian Islands

Within Hawaii's sun-warmed shallows, Nature has put on a truly breathtaking display of one of its most ambitious and prolific creations — the teeming world of the coral reef. Hawaii offers the full gamut of underwater experiences. Hawaii even boasts its own "ghost fleet": scattered across the reef floor of many islands are numerous sunken wrecks — ships, boats, and even planes — sent to a watery grave by storms and other maritime mishaps.

Water Conditions. Hawaiian shores feel the brunt of all kinds of wind, wave, and water conditions. Currents are perhaps the greatest concern. Some diving areas, particularly those on the leeward coasts, are almost always free of any noticeable currents, while other areas may be plagued by swiftly moving waters practically all year. The Hawaiian Islands are relatively young, geologically speaking, and the corals have not yet had time to build protective fringing reefs. Without these natural breakwaters, many shorelines are pounded by the full fury of the Pacific Ocean.

A popular way to visit Hawaii's shallow-water reefs is by boat. Vessels range in size from smaller "6-pack" dive boats to large catamarans, which offer lunch and a variety of watersports from spacious decks.

Wind. Wind direction plays a vital role in determining day-to-day diving conditions. Eighty percent of the time the tradewinds blow from the northeast, and the calmer waters of leeward coastlines generally make for the best year-round diving. A word of caution, however: the wind shadow (the sheltered area protected from wind contact) generally extends only a few hundred yards (200-300 meters) offshore, where the trades once again hit the water and produce a surface current that flows out to sea. When you make a beach dive, be sure to leave sufficient air to enable you to swim back inside the wind shadow before you surface.

In the winter months (November to April), the trades sometimes die down and are replaced by southerly Kona winds. The strength of these winds has a profound effect on diving areas, especially those on leeward coasts. When the Kona winds gust up from the south, high surf makes these areas undiveable. When the trades are replaced by Kona weather, divers flock to the windward side to log some bottom time during the temporary calm. Occasionally the Konas are very weak (less than 5 knots) and tranquil waters prevail almost everywhere.

On several islands the land forms protective wind shadows on the north shores and, during the summer months, these waters are calm and extremely popular among underwater enthusiasts. In the winter, however, the north shores become home to giant surf, and a number of treacherous rips and undertows — not to mention big waves — make diving hazardous. Dives should then be restricted to more protected locales.

Long-time island divers familiar with such perversities of wind, weather, and water know where and when to dive certain spots. If you are new to Hawaiian waters, you need to acquaint yourself with the variable conditions in order to maximize your enjoyment and diving safety.

Drop-offs. The well-defined ledges that run parallel to shore are among the most notable underwater features found around many of the islands. They are called drop-offs and are located anywhere from near the shore to several hundred yards (200–300 meters) or more out. Such drop-offs create interesting topography, with steep walls cut by spectacular ravines, dramatic caves, and huge grottos that bustle with marine life.

Sport Diving Options

There are two ways to explore Hawaii's underwater realm: on your own or with a dive charter tour. A complete range of tour packages is available on most islands, from the normal half-day and full-day beach or boat excursions to special overnight or extended tours aboard larger dive vessels. All scuba divers who want to rent gear, fill tanks, or join a dive tour must present a certification card. Intro dives are particularly

Snorkeling in Hawaii's shallow, clear waters is easy and can be enjoyed by young and old alike.

popular among visiting divers. In this case, no prior certification is required and intro divers are assigned to an instructor who first teaches the basics of scuba diving techniques and equipment, then takes the intro diver on a personally escorted tour of the reef. There is no type of certification required to rent or purchase skin diving gear (mask, snorkel, and fins) or to participate in snorkel tours.

Scuba Diving. If you have never been scuba diving, there are two ways to get started. You can take an intro scuba dive if your time (or funds) are limited, which involves basic instruction followed by an underwater tour in the company of a professional instructor and underwater guide. It's an easy, inexpensive way to get a taste of scuba diving and to see if you are interested in taking a complete certification course.

For those who wish to get more seriously involved with the scuba sport, dive shops and scuba tour companies offer special courses that last only five days. The graduating student earns a certification card that can be used to buy and rent gear and have tanks filled anywhere in the world.

Snorkeling. Although a great many visitors enjoy scuba diving in Hawaii, a great many more people see the underwater world with only mask, snorkel, and flippers. If you are diving on your own, decide whether you or others traveling with you will be snorkeling, scuba diving, or mixing the two; then choose a dive site in this book accordingly. For instance, don't choose a spot that is indicated as being good only for scuba if there are snorkelers in your group. It is easy enough to choose a spot where both can enjoy the water.

Tour Companies

Whether you wish to go skin or scuba diving alone, or if you elect to go with an organized tour, there are different kinds of companies from which you can choose.

Equipment Rental Companies. In well-developed areas, such as Honolulu and Waikiki on Oahu; Lahaina, Kaanapali, and Kihei on Maui; Kona on Hawaii; or Poipu, Kapaa, and Hanalei on Kauai, a myriad of companies rent all kinds of gear, from snorkeling sets by the day or the week to float boards with underwater viewing ports, floatation devices, and underwater cameras. These outfits generally don't rent scuba equipment. Furthermore, they only rent the gear and you must supply your own transportation to and from the dive site. Some companies, however, also rent mopeds, which are useful for traveling short distances.

Shuttle Companies. Some shuttle companies rent snorkeling gear and offer transportation service to and from selected dive sites, primarily very popular snorkeling dive sites such as famous Hanauma Bay on Oahu. Most of these companies only rent snorkel gear and underwater cameras. They do not supply any sort of scuba equipment, instruction, or underwater guided tours.

Dive Shops. These generally specialize in scuba-diving tours only, though a few combine both skin- and scuba-diving activities. Most dive

Molokini Crater near Maui is one of the more scenic — both above and below water — and interesting diving sites found anywhere in Hawaii.

shops operate dive boats to transport divers to better, offshore areas. Some places do specialize in beach diving, such as around Hanauma Bay on Oahu, and the well-known Black Rock dive site near the Sheraton Hotel in Kaanapali. Most shops, though, rent both scuba and snorkeling equipment, including underwater cameras.

Big Boats. Some companies, particularly those running their trips on large boats (especially the big catamarans) offer a mixture of snorkeling and scuba tours. Waikiki, Kaneohe Bay, Lahaina, Kaanapali, Kihei, Kona, and other areas feature numerous vessels that visit the most beautiful beaches and reefs in the islands.

Fish and Game Regulations. You should be aware of some regulations established by the Division of Fish and Game concerning the collecting of various types of marine life.

1. Octopus less than 1 pound (2.2 kilograms) may not be taken.
2. Spiny and slipper lobsters may be taken only from September to May 1, and they must weigh more than 1 pound (2.2 kilograms). Females with eggs can't be collected, nor may you use a spear for collecting purposes.
3. Collecting tropical fish for aquarium use reuires a special license. No license is required for sportfishing, and the season is open all year.
4. No collecting of any kind is allowed in prescribed marine parks and sanctuaries. Such areas are well marked by signs.
5. No taking of live corals is allowed in less than 30 feet (10 meters) of water and within 1,000 feet (300 meters) from shore.

More complete details on these and other regulations can be obtained from the local Division of Fish and Game office.

◀ *Molokini — which can only be reached by boat — is visited daily by boats carrying both scuba divers and snorkeling enthusiasts.*

3

Diving Oahu

Oahu contains the greatest abundance of snorkel- and scuba-oriented services and facilities in the state. Equipment rentals and air fills are easily available all around the island, and there are many charter companies that specialize in underwater guided tours. The majority of shops and

Oahu, with the capital city of Honolulu and the beach at Waikiki, is the center of population and tourism in Hawaii. Development and good diving coexist at many points around the island.

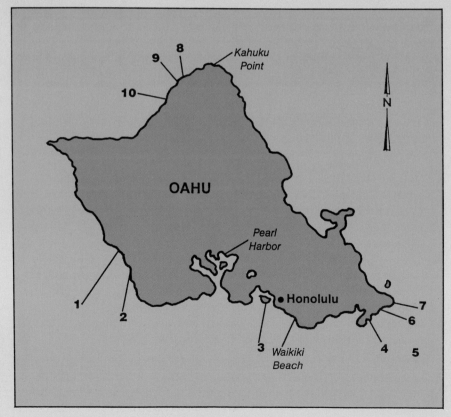

Dive Site Ratings

	Novice Diver	Novice Diver with Instructor or Divemaster	Intermediate Diver	Intermediate Diver with Instructor or Divemaster	Advanced Diver	Advanced Diver with Instructor or Divemaster
Oahu						
1 Mahi Boat Dive			x	x	x	x
2 Kahe Point Beach Park*						
(novice in shore)	x	x	x	x	x	x
3 Magic Island			x	x	x	x
4 Hanauma Bay*						
(novice on inner reef)			x	x	x	x
5 Pinnacle outside						
Hanauma Bay					x	x
6 Blowhole			x	x	x	x
7 Sandy Beach			x	x	x	x
8 Shark's Cove (Pupukea)	x	x	x	x	x	x
9 Three Tables			x	x	x	x
10 Waimea Bay*	x	x	x	x	x	x

* Indicates good snorkeling spot

When using this chart, see the information on pages 1-2 for an explanation of the diver rating system and site locations.

dive facilities are concentrated in the Honolulu and Waikiki areas, with others scattered throughout the island.

Oahu's sheltered leeward coastline, which extends from Kaena Point to Diamond Head, is perhaps the most popular overall diving area because of its nearly year-round accessibility. In the tradewind shadow of the Waianae and Koolau mountains, waters tend to be calmer. The coastline is nearly uninterrupted beach from Barber's Point to Kaena Point, but you have to hit the right places to find any reefs.

Extending from Diamond Head to Makapuu Point is a craggy, panoramic coastline characterized by sheer sea cliffs and an oftentimes pounding surf. This area also feels the grip of a treacherous current known as the "Molokai Express." Slow-moving ocean currents funnel between

Molokai and Oahu and result in a venturi effect that speeds water movement to as much as 5 knots. The Molokai Express is weakest near shore, so stay in close when diving this area.

On this side of Oahu you'll also find Hanauma Bay, one of the most scenic spots in all the islands. The remains of an ancient volcanic crater now open to the sea at one side, secluded Hanauma Bay is the perfect spot for seasoned and novice divers alike. There is a shallow inner reef for swimming and snorkeling and an outer reef that offers deeper, clearer waters.

The windward side of Oahu extends from Makapuu Point to Kahuku. Diving conditions are excellent during Kona weather on the offshore reefs. This side of the island, however, is generally under the influence of the normal tradewinds, and the water is too rough for diving most of the year.

The north shore of Oahu is a ribbon of wide, sandy beaches adorned by inland coves and bays. During the summer months the high surf is on vacation and the area becomes a diver's paradise. It is a good area for the beginner.

Oahu's sheltered Hanauma Bay is one of the most popular and easily accessible skin and scuba diving sites in all of Hawaii.

Typical Depth Range:	90 feet (28 meters) to the bottom; about 60 feet (18 meters) on the top of the wreck
Typical Current Conditions:	Mild to nonexistent during normal weather
Expertise Required:	Intermediate to advanced
Access:	Boat

The waters around the Hawaiian Islands contain a number of sunken wrecks that have become artificial reefs — man-made products that have sunk in shallow water and become the home for a myriad of colorful and fascinating marine creatures. Most of these artificial reefs are the result of accidents: derelict remains of World War II in the Pacific, maritime mishaps, or the sometimes violent moods of weather.

In 1982 the first planned artificial reef was created: the *M/V Mahi*. The *Mahi*, a 165-foot (50-meter), 600-ton vessel, was originally built for the Navy. It was later converted to an oceanographic research ship used by the University of Hawaii. No longer seaworthy, it was due to be sunk off Honolulu in deep water. Hearing of this, local divers intervened and, with the help of volunteers, had the plans changed so that the *Mahi* was sunk in shallow water as Hawaii's first planned artificial reef.

The Mahi wreck, the state's first planned artificial reef, has become a popular residence for many reef creatures. Multihued encrusting sponges, corals, and other growth provide homes for a wide variety of fish life. Rays and sea turtles are frequently seen nearby.

The *Mahi* is now one of the best, and certainly the most accessible, intact sunken wrecks in the state. It is located about 1 mile (1½ kilometers) offshore of Maile point and is visited by several dive tours on a daily basis (weather permitting).

Even for seasoned wreck divers, the *Mahi* is exciting. Whether just a sightseer or an experienced underwater photographer, there's lots to see and do. Most of the external superstructure is covered with colorful encrusting sponges, corals, and innumerable fish. Schools of friendly, curious lemon-yellow butterflyfish create spectacular scenery and great picture-taking opportunities.

Also usually found on the bottom towards the stern is one of many resident moray eels. Some 4 feet long, this individual is easily hand-fed — even held and petted — by divers with such inclinations.

There is also a lot to explore inside the *Mahi*, but be sure to bring along a flashlight. Do not, however, enter areas where you cannot see light marking a clear exit path. It is dangerous to penetrate wrecks without special training; make sure you are with an expert before entering the *Mahi*.

The *Mahi* is best dived between tides when the current is at a minimum.

The exotic lionfish, a member of the scorpionfish family, is beautiful but deadly. It is not commonly seen in Hawaii, and is usually only found at night in the recesses of darker caves, and sometimes in the deeper interior of the Mahi.

Typical Depth Range:	20–30 feet (6–10 meters)
Typical Current Conditions:	Mild to nonexistent in the wind shadow, except during Kona weather
Expertise Required:	Beginner near shore, advanced farther out near ledge
Access:	Beach

The Kahe Point Beach Park is located at approximately 89-620 Farrington Highway 90. The entrance is marked by a sign on the highway. It is an excellent spot for a family or group outing, with swimming and snorkeling, as well as scuba diving, in calm, shallow water relatively near to shore.

Diving is not good off the beach park itself, as the bottom is mostly sand. The best spot to enter and exit is to the east of the beach (left side of the parking lot as you face the water) from a small rocky cove.

Known for its abundance of sea turtles, Kahe Point features patches of corals on a white sand bottom in shallow, calm waters.

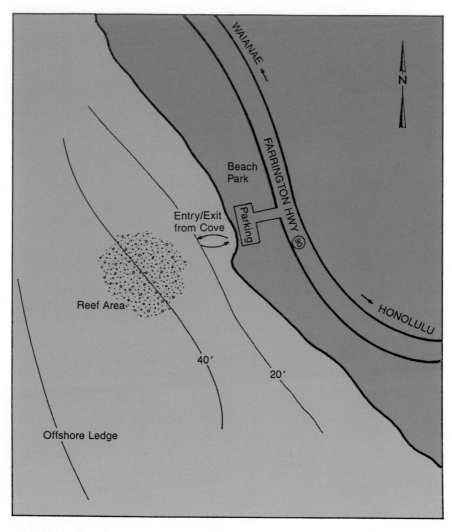

Kahe Point Beach Park is an excellent spot for a family or group outing, with swimming, snorkeling, and scuba diving available.

The bottom slopes very gently out from shore and for a long way is only about 20 feet (6 meters) deep. Near shore, the bottom is mostly sand and large coral heads, but this develops into a lush coral reef further offshore. This is, in fact, one of the most extensive coral reefs on Oahu and, because it is in shallow water, it is great for less-experienced skin and scuba enthusiasts.

Underwater Scenery. For the first several dozen yards or so you will see mostly sand, and visibility tends to be rather poor. Beyond this point are coral patches separated by sand, and good visibility as you reach the coral reefs. Beginners and intermediate divers should stay within 200 yards (185 meters) of shore to keep within the protective wind shadow, but the experienced diver may wish to travel farther offshore. Some 400 yards (370 meters) out, the depth is around 60 feet (18 meters) and visibility usually 100 feet (30 meters) or more. Out here you will find an interesting offshore ledge, pockmarked with small grottos that are home to many fish and other smaller marine life. The area is also known among local divers for its abundance of turtles. Sharks are sometimes sighted here.

Caution. If you do venture out this far, be certain to leave sufficient air for a return trip underwater. Ideally, you should get to within the wind shadow before you have to surface.

Kahe Point Beach Park, far from crowded Waikiki, is one of Oahu's most secluded beaches.

Typical Depth Range:	20–50 feet (6–15 meters)
Typical Current Conditions:	Some near-shore surge, but little current except during Kona winds
Expertise Required:	Intermediate to advanced
Access:	Beach

The lovely sheltered beach and swimming area of Ala Moana Beach Park (adjacent to this site) lets non-divers enjoy themselves while the old salts explore the underwater world.

Entry and exit are most convenient from the Magic Island cove. Within the first 100 yards (90 meters) or shore, the depth averages 20–30 feet (6–10 meters), with a visibility averaging 40–50 feet (12–15 meters). The bottom terrain is mostly hard rock, with small caves found running between the many surge channels. A little further offshore the visibility

The protection offered by its thick, strong spines allows the red slate-urchin to remain out in the open during the day while many other small reef creatures are hiding from predators.

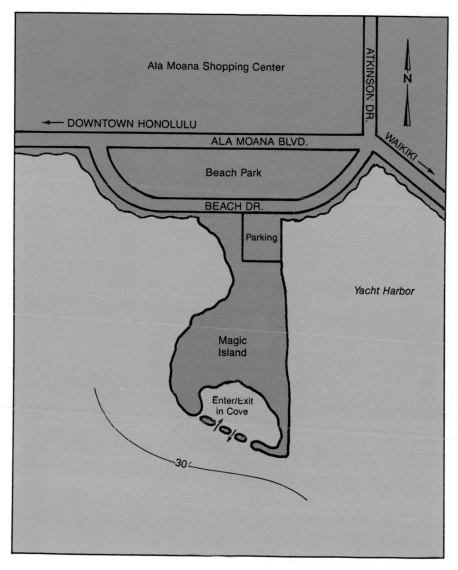

With its close access to the Ala Moana Shopping Center and pleasant beach park, the Magic Island dive site offers something for everyone.

improves; at a depth of 50 feet (15 meters), sand and coral formations predominate.

Admittedly, Magic Island is not the best dive site on Oahu. However, it is very easily reached, as it is located on the western edge of Waikiki. Ala Moana Beach Park is perhaps the nicest beach park on Oahu, and is

Although Magic Island is not one of Oahu's premiere dive sites, it is conveniently reached, makes a lovely spot for a family outing, and does have some nice underwater scenery, especially for the newcomer to the underwater world.

right across the street from Ala Moana Shopping Center. Magic Island is a popular dive site with visitors and locals alike because of its overall convenience: close to town with excellent facilities, and nice underwater sights as well. It's perfect for the more casual diver traveling with family or friends who do not wish to visit more remote dive sites or spend the day waiting for the divers to get out of the water. At Magic Island and Ala Moana, there is literally something for everyone.

Typical Depth Range:	10 feet (3 meters) on the inner reef, sloping to 70 feet (23 meters) at the mouth of the bay
Typical Current Conditions:	Generally nonexistent
Expertise Required:	Novice on the inner reef; intermediate to advanced on the outer reef
Access:	Beach

Hanauma Bay is one of the most beautiful spots in all the tropical Pacific. It is one of those panoramic extravaganzas of nature which must be seen to be believed. If you do nothing else on Oahu, visit Hanauma Bay. Even if you only peer over the scenic lookout (you won't be able to take your eyes away for some time), the sight will make your day.

Today, Hanauma Bay is one of the most sheltered coastal areas in the state. Only when oddball winds blow up out of the southeast (only a few

On the outer reef at Hanauma Bay, a soldierfish nestles in the hollow of a rock coated with encrusting sponges.

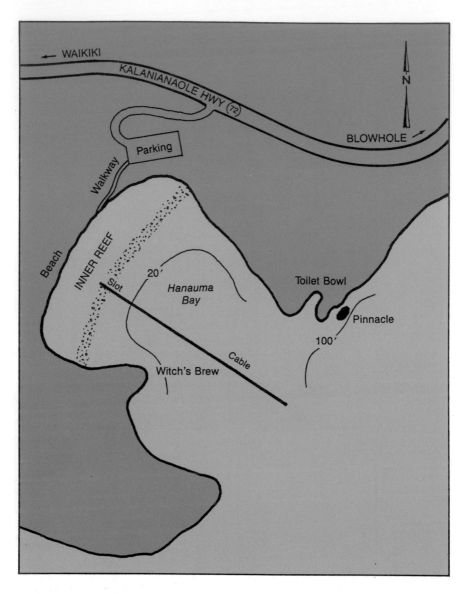

Hanauma Bay is one of the most sheltered coastal areas in the state, while the Pinnacle outside the bay requires more advanced scuba skills.

days a year) is the water rough and poor for diving. Most of the time it is ideal for family and group outings. Because it is such a popular spot, a large number of dive-tour and shuttle companies run trips daily to the bay from Waikiki.

The Inner Reef. There are two diving areas within the bay. The first is the inner reef, which is like a giant saltwater swimming pool and is almost always calm. Swimming is excellent here in the several large sandy-bottom tide pools created within the reef itself. The maximum depth of the inner reef is about 10 feet (3 meters) depending on tide. Visibility runs anywhere from good to poor depending on daily conditions of water movement and how many people are kicking about and stirring up the sand. In general, morning offers the clearest, least crowded diving. There is little coral in this area, but the volcanic rock topography is nice. The unique thing about the inner reef is the fish — there are so many of them! The fish, such as lemon butterflyfish, convict tangs, and parrotfish, are extremely plentiful here and very tame because all of Hanauma Bay is a protected marine park — so tame, in fact, they will eat right out of your hand! The inner reef is ideal for the beginning snorkeler and scuba diver.

The Outer Reef. For the more experienced snorkeler and scuba enthusiast, the outer reef is a veritable underwater playground. The outer

Witch's Brew is perhaps the nicest of the dive sites in Hanauma Bay's outer-reef area. It's a great spot for underwater photography.

reef slopes gradually from about 13 feet (5 meters) to around 70 feet (21 meters) near the mouth of the bay. Literally all areas of the bay, from just outside the inner barrier reef to the mouth of the bay, are filled with lush coral gardens, an abundance of fish, turtles, and other interesting creatures.

For exploring just outside the inner reef and partway out into the bay, intermediate skills are recommended. Only advanced divers should venture far out into the bay and to the mouth. This area does have some beautiful diving, but the water is deeper, currents develop, and you will be quite far from shore for the return swim.

The Slot. To leave the inner reef and reach the outer bay, do not try and swim over the barrier reef. This is dangerous due to waves washing across the surface of the rocks. There is a passage through the reef, known as "the slot", which creates a convenient entry and exit to the inner reef. The slot is located to the right side of the bay out from the lifeguard stand. A large cable runs through this channel and can be followed a good distance out into the bay, and makes a convenient guide back into the inner reef at the completion of the dive. The outer reef can also be entered from the right hand (or Witch's Brew) side by walking along the

Hanauma Bay is the very picture of a tropical South Seas lagoon. The inner reef — the dark patches of rocks and coral in the foreground — is excellent for novice scuba divers and snorkelers. The outer reef provides greater depth and visibility and is recommended for the more experienced diver.

reef perimeter. This is a longer walk with heavy gear on, but does involve much less of a swim once in the water.

Witch's Brew. Although the bay offers good diving in many areas, there is a particularly interesting spot on the right-hand side close to shore. To the right, out along the crescent arm of the crater wall, is a small peninsula that juts out from shore. In front of this peninsula is a lush coral reef and huge surge channels that create some exciting diving and scenic topography. This area is known as Witch's Brew because several different wave and current patterns merge at this point. The result is turbulent surface waters and back-and-forth surging currents on the bottom down to about 30 feet (10 meters). Most of the time the currents are not severe, but they do tend to move you around and care must be taken not to get scraped across the sharp coral.

Underwater Photography. Hanauma Bay is one of the best spots in the state to get some really nice underwater photos. The clear water and varied seascapes produce excellent diver scenics (photos with divers in the scene), while the plentiful and friendly fish offer the best in close-up photography.

Typical Depth Range:	20 feet (6 meters) on top, deeper down sides
Typical Current Conditions:	Calmest at slack tide. Current picks up strongly as tide changes "Molokai Express"
Expertise Required:	Advanced
Access:	Boat

The pinnacle is located just outside the mouth of Hanauma Bay — to the right as you look into the bay from the ocean side. The top of the pinnacle is rather flat, lacking in interesting topographic features. Boat anchoring is best done on the top of the pinnacle. Inspect the anchor line to be certain it is well set; currents can come up swiftly and suddenly as the tides change and it is easy for a boat to drag anchor.

Because of the sweeping currents, the top of the pinnacle does not have a lot of significant coral growth or marine life. As you swim toward the edge, the flat top gives way to a dramatic drop-off. The flanks around the pinnacle tend to be sheer precipices extending down to very deep water. There is a shallower bridge connecting the pinnacle to the nearby coastline. Being in an open-ocean environment (which experiences significant water movement), visibility tends to be quite good, often well in excess of 100 feet.

At varying locations and depths surrounding the pinnacle are ledges and caves that break up the steep cliffs. Marine life is abundant and on any dive you are likely to see a good representation of Hawaiian marine flora and fauna. Caves and grottos are painted with colorful encrusting sponges, bright coral polyps, and invertebrates such as nudibranchs, sea shells, starfish, and the like. Fish life is plentiful. Especially photogenic are the large schools of Moorish idols, butterflyfish, and their relatives. Turtles and larger fish are also seen there, including reef white-tip sharks and, every once in awhile, a hammerhead shark cruising by.

The Pinnacle is characterized by sheer walls, ledges, caves, and abundant marine life. ▶

Typical Depth Range:	20–60 feet (6–18 meters)
Typical Current Conditions:	Generally little current within 100 yards (90 meters) of shore; "Molokai Express" farther out
Expertise Required:	Intermediate to advanced
Access:	Beach

A secluded beach little known to visitors but popular among locals is the cove near the Blowhole lookout. If you take the coastal Kalaianaole Highway 72 past Hanauma Bay, you will come to a sign indicating the Blowhole lookout. Park in this area. To the right of the parking lot (as you face the ocean) is a path leading down to the beach. There are no public facilities, but the beach is nice for sunbathing before or after the dive. Much of the year the surf is mild and you can follow the underwater corridor out of the cove into some interesting diving.

The area is characterized by patches of rock and coral with sand stretches in-between. Visibility is poor close to shore due to wave action, but the bottom slopes gently from about 15 feet (5 meters) at the mouth of the cove and the water clarity becomes much better farther offshore. The best diving is found to the right as you swim outside the cove. It becomes deeper at a much greater rate here than it does going straight out or to

The Blowhole Cove is found to the right of the parking lot. The beach makes a convenient entry and exit location.

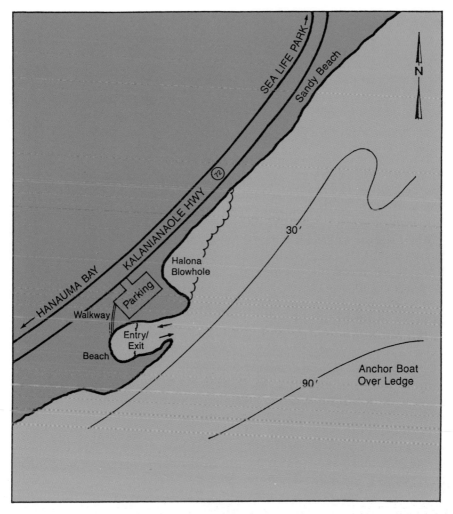

Access to the Blowhole site is via the beach, but do not attempt a beach dive from Sandy Beach as it is notorious for crashing waves with a dangerous shore break.

the left of the cove. This deeper area to the right features some fascinating ledges and cliffs, one of which drops straight down from 20 to 60 feet (8 to 18 meters).

Although the small beach affords safe entry and exit, care should be taken when going through the waves because there are rocks. Also remember the Molokai Express offshore — it can be a treacherous and unforgiving current if you venture too far out. Stay within 100 yards (90 meters) of the shore and, to be on the safe side, try and dive Blowhole only at a slack or incoming tide.

Typical Depth Range:	50–90 feet
Typical Current Conditions:	Generally milder current nearer to shore; "Molokai Express" farther out
Expertise Required:	Intermediate to advanced
Access:	Boat

Not far past the Blowhole, to the east around the coastline, is Sandy Beach. Offshore there are some nice diving spots. The only safe access here is by boat. *Do not* be tempted to make a shore dive. Sandy Beach is a well-known, rather notorious surfing beach typified by waves with a dangerous shore break.

The offshore ledge lies several hundred yards out in about 70 to 90 feet of water. A depth sounder is very handy for locating this ledge. Running from ledge to shoreline, the bottom gradually gets shallower but turbidity due to beach wave action makes diving best at 50 feet or greater depths. For shallower spots, the previously described and nearby Blowhole dive site is recommended.

The offshore Sandy Beach spot is characterized by rock and coral. There is nice topography in many areas, with caverns, caves, and scenic drop-offs. Fish, such as lemon butterflyfish, nempachi, parrotfish, and Moorish idols, are plentiful, and turtles are often sighted here. This is a particularly good photographic location for underwater shots of fish and smaller invertebrate marine life, as well as nice diver scenics.

Although this dive site does not tend to possess the sheer scenic topography and impressive drop-offs found at the Hanauma Bay pinnacle, diving conditions are easier and currents are not as severe. Whereas the tides must be carefully chosen for a pinnacle dive, the Sandy Beach area is less current sensitive with tidal shifts.

Sandy Beach diving offers nice topographic relief with plentiful marine life.

Typical Depth Range:	20–50 feet (6–15 meters) near shore, sloping gradually deeper
Typical Current Conditions:	Hazardous during winter; generally calm during summer
Expertise Required:	Novice to intermediate
Access:	Beach

Shark's Cove was not named for the presence of its toothy namesake, but because some imaginative diver thought certain of the rocks there resembled a shark.

Also known as Pupukea, Shark's Cove is perhaps the most popular of all north shore dive sites. During the months from about May to October it is almost always calm, with little if any current or significant wave action. Thus, it is an excellent spot for beginning divers to sharpen their underwater skills. It is also popular with more advanced divers because of the labyrinthine network of undersea caves and caverns.

Actually, good diving is not found within the cove itself, but outside it. Entry and exit from the water, however, are most conveniently accomplished from the sandy beach that rings the cove. After a brief swim outside the cove to the right you will find the first cave mouth in about

One entrance to the underwater caves at Shark's Cove can be found in the shoreline reef to the right of the cove itself. The most convenient — in terms of walking — way to reach the caves, however, is by entering the water in the cove and swimming out.

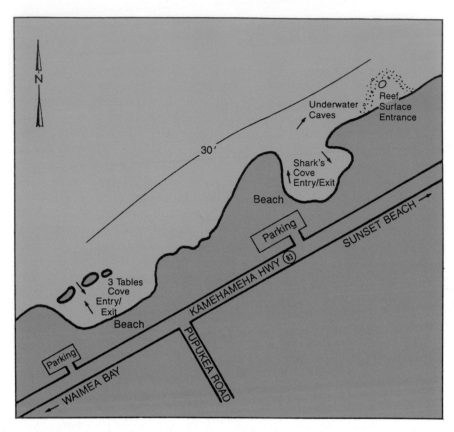

Shark's Cove is an excellent place for beginning divers to sharpen their skills, while Three Tables is better left to more advanced divers.

20 feet (6 meters) of water. Visibility is poor in the cove but improves immediately outside.

Underwater Terrain. Approximately 100 yards (90 meters) past the mouth of Shark's Cove and to the right, you will come upon caverns of varying sizes carved under the volcanic-rock shoreline. The great majority of caves and passageways run a few dozen feet (about 8–12 meters) before opening out into the blue water again, and make for fascinating exploration. Some caves, on the other hand, penetrate deep back into the rock. These should be reserved only for the experienced and knowledgeable cave diver, and you should never penetrate so deeply as to lose sight of the entrance. Also, when entering a cavern, remember that the water will be clear at first, but as you penetrate further, sand and silt tend to be stirred up by kicking fins and bubble exhalations, and the entrance can be quickly obscured. **Caution is the watchword when entering any underwater cave, no matter how shallow it may be. Novice divers should not penetrate deeper than just inside a cave entrance unless accompanied by a professional tour guide or instructor.** Additionally, even if you are an advanced diver, you should check the surge conditions that day. Before entering a cave, swim around outside for a few minutes to see how the surge currents are behaving. During the summer months most days will be calm, but on some days there will be strong water surges that can throw you helplessly about inside a cave if you are not extremely careful.

Parrotfish, active during the day, back themselves into protective cubbyholes during the night. After bedding down, some individuals surround themselves with a secretion that forms a thin, translucent bubble.

Cave Diving

Exploring underwater caves is fascinating, but it can be dangerous without proper instruction and should only be attempted after receiving special training. When cave diving, you should keep the following points in mind:

1. Never enter a cave without a diving buddy.
2. Always check weather conditions to be sure the surf is down, as this will indicate milder water movement for safer cave entry. Do not enter caves if there is strong water movement.
3. Use a safety line to help find the way back out of a cave.
4. Always take a flashlight into caves.

Night Diving. If you are a night diver, Shark's Cove is a great spot to visit during the summer months. The best way to dive this area at night is to swim out and find the dive site just before sundown. For night diving, the area to the left of the cove is recommended. There are no caves here but a much greater quantity of marine life for after-dark sightseeing. This is a particularly good area for underwater photography at night — the black background water produces an excellent contrast to the bright yellow coral polyps, flame-orange crabs, multicolored nudibranchs and sea shells, big-eyed squirrelfish, and much more.

Night diving at Shark's Cove is recommended only for the advanced diver experienced in the exploration of the water world after dark. Near shore the depths do not exceed 50 feet (15 meters), and it is important not to lose track of the mouth of the cove, which is the only good place to exit from the water as the rest of the surrounding coastline is rugged wave-washed lava rock.

Before attempting a night dive at Shark's Cove, it is best to check recent weather and water conditions with a dive shop, and the weather forecast for the night with the weather service. Only dive the area at night if the surf is down, the weather is good, and the water in the cove is calm. With a little caution, a night dive at Shark's Cove can be one of the highlights of your Hawaiian diving experience.

Typical Depth Range:	20–60 feet (6–18 meters)
Typical Current Conditions:	Hazardous during winter; generally calm during summer
Expertise Required:	Intermediate to advanced
Access:	Beach

Three Tables is less than 1 mile (1½ kilometers) down the road from Shark's Cove, on the way to Waimea Bay on Kamehameha Highway 83. Three Tables is a superior dive site to Waimea in terms of underwater terrain and marine life, but it requires a slightly higher skill level.

Three Tables is so named because of offshore ledges that produce really spectacular seascapes featuring arches, overhangs, and large crevasses. The best entry and exit points are along the rocky shoreline in front of the parking area. Due to wave action, this shoreline does require caution, however, when getting in and out of the water. Visibility tends to be rather good near shore and gets steadily better the further out you swim. The bottom is very rocky, sloping gently outward.

A diver feeds a small spotted moray eel during a dive. Even heavy gloves are no match for the eel's sharp teeth, and such hand-feeding is not really recommended.

Another colorful reef inhabitant active at night is the lobster. A relative of the larger — and somewhat tastier — Maine lobster, this species lacks the crusher claws.

Near-shore depths run around 20–30 feet (6–10 meters), and the area is characterized by large pot-hole depressions in the rock substrate with many interconnecting tunnels and passageways.

The best locations for diving are not straight offshore but to the right, found by swimming out diagonally in the direction of Shark's Cove. It's a fairly long swim of 15 to 20 minutes and is best done on the surface, snorkeling to conserve air. At a distance of 100–200 yards (90–180 meters) offshore, the water is the clearest, with the depth averaging 60 feet (18 meters). It's a great lobster area because of the caverns, lava tubes, huge overhangs, and the like. Large conger eels are frequently spotted here, along with a varied marine population of fish, nudibranchs, crustaceans, and so on.

Typical Depth Range:	10–30 feet (3–10 meters)
Typical Current Conditions:	Dangerous surf and currents during winter months; generally calm during summer
Expertise Required:	Novice
Access:	Beach

Next to Hanauma Bay, Waimea Bay may be the most picturesque beach on Oahu, certainly on the north shore. Even if you are a two-tank diver and make your two dives at Shark's Cove and Three Tables, Waimea is a great place to finish the day with a picnic and relaxation.

Good Novice Diving. Waimea is not recommended for the intermediate and advanced diver simply because it doesn't offer the underwater scenery

The large eyes of the squirrelfish mark it as another nocturnal creature. During the day, they can usually be found in shady recesses under reefs or rocks.

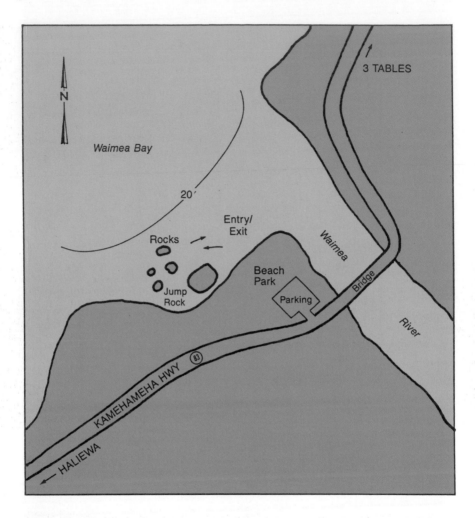

Waimea Bay may be the most picturesque beach on Oahu, and is highly recommended for novice divers.

and marine life of other dive sites. Waimea, on the other hand, is highly recommended for novice divers who wish to log some bottom time in calm, easily diveable waters. The spot to go is on the left side of the bay, out around the big rocks. This area is very near shore, requiring only a short, easy swim. Near shore the water surge may or may not throw you around a bit, depending on the day. The visibility is normally not the best, as you are in so close in only 10 or 15 feet (3–5 meters) of water. A little further offshore, but still within a few hundred feet (60–90

The rocks at the left are the best dive site at Waimea Bay. The bay is calm and a good site for beginners, but only during the calm summer months!

meters), the depth increases to 20 feet (6 meters) or more and visibility improves.

Underwater Scenery and Marine Life. This area is strewn with large volcanic boulders ranging anywhere from less than 1 foot (30 centimeters) to many feet, with some large ones being 10 feet (3 meters) or more in diameter. There is little coral growth on the rocks; the rest of the area is sand sloping gradually outward from the beach. The marine life consists of small tropical fish but not a lot of growth, because during the winter months huge surf, up to 40 feet (12 meters) high, pounds the rocks. Waimea is an excellent novice snorkeling place; again, not so much for the scenery but because it is such a calm, easy spot to dive. Great for kids and other folks who may not feel really comfortable in the water but would still like to see something of the underwater world.

4

Diving Maui

Maui offers top-notch dive shops and underwater tour companies in Kaanapali, Lahaina, and Kihei/Wailea. The longest coastline on Maui is the north shore, but it is infrequently dived because of its remoteness and the year-round rough waters. The windward southeast shore is also generally off limits because of winds, swells, and currents.

With a variety of hotel and .beachfront dive operations from which to choose, Maui offers very convenient diving both around the island and at nearby Molokini Crater and Lanai Island.

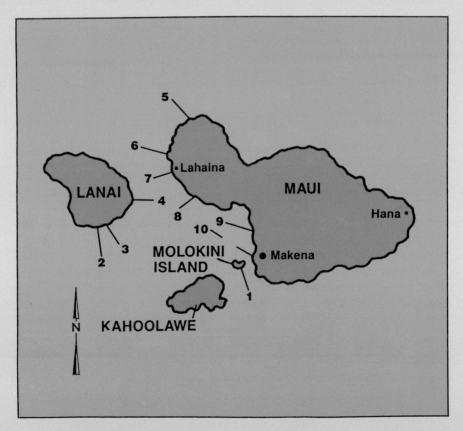

Dive Site Ratings

	Novice Diver	Novice Diver with Instructor or Divemaster	Intermediate Diver	Intermediate Diver with Instructor or Divemaster	Advanced Diver	Advanced Diver with Instructor or Divemaster
Maui						
1 Molokini Crater* (novice in shallow water)					x	x
2 Lanai Island— Hulopoe Bay*	x	x	x	x	x	x
3 Lanai Island— the Cathedrals					x	x
4 Lanai Island— Turtle Dive		x	x	x	x	x
5 Honolua Bay*	x	x	x	x	x	x
6 Black Rock* (novice inside sheltered lagoon)			x	x	x	x
7 Lahaina*	x	x	x	x	x	x
8 Olowalu*	x	x	x	x	x	x
9 Wailea Beach* (novice inshore)			x	x	x	x
10 Makena Beach			x	x	x	x

* Indicates good snorkeling spot

When using this chart, see the information on pages 1-2 for an explanation of the diver rating system and site locations.

Maui's leeward shore, from La Perouse to Kaanapali, has the best diving. Many hotels have a beach activities operation that provides every service from renting dive gear, to teaching snorkeling and scuba diving, to signing you up for boat trips to nearby islands.

Actually, some of the better diving is not found on Maui proper but on the nearby islet of Molokini and the south and southeast shores of Lanai island. Dive sites for these islands are also covered in this chapter.

From November to April, you might be able to catch one of the biggest thrills Maui's marine world has to offer: seeing first-hand the mammoth humpback whales that migrate to Hawaii each year. Even if you don't catch a glimpse of them, you'll know the gentle giants are nearby; once underwater you can hear their pleasant song echoing as they communicate with each other.

Typical Depth Range:	10 feet (3 meters) near shore to about 60–90 feet (18–27 meters) at the drop-off
Typical Current Conditions:	Mild or non-existent during the morning; strong in the afternoon
Expertise Required:	Novice in shallow near-shore waters to advanced in deep water and over the drop-off
Access:	Boat

Molokini is a small islet, actually the tip of a small extinct volcanic crater barely ¼ mile (400 meters) long, rising out of the blue Pacific between Maui and Kahoolawe. One half of the crater is still intact above water, the other half having long since been eroded away. Molokini is 45 minutes to an hour away from Maui by boat. The attractions: a panoramic view that takes in no less than 5 of the 8 major Hawaiian islands; majestic coral formations; spectacular walls and drop-offs; whale and porpoise watching; and schools of tame tropical fish that can be hand-fed. This dive spot comes highly recommended!

Both snorkeling and scuba are terrific at Molokini. Snorkelers generally find the shallow, inner near-shore crater waters more calm and thus best for surface swimming. Depth here ranges anywhere from 10–30 feet (3–10 meters), with the bottom sloping down gradually to 60–90 feet (18–27 meters) near the ledges. Scuba diving boats frequently anchor to the left side opposite the lighthouse, where the bottom terrain goes from

Maui features many scenic coastal areas. Here is a string of white beach on the protected leeward shore along the road to Lahaina.

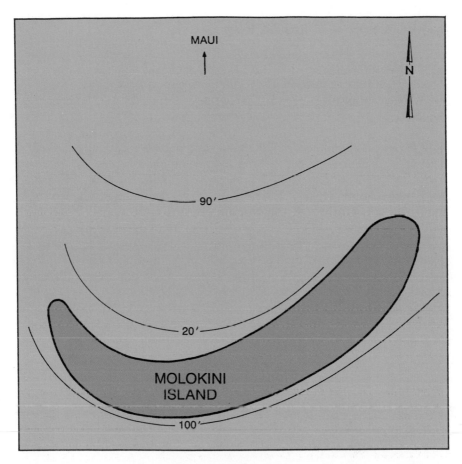

MAUI

N

90'

20'

MOLOKINI
ISLAND

100'

Both snorkeling and scuba are terrific at Molokini, with its panoramic views, majestic coral formations, spectacular walls and drop-offs, whale and porpoise watching, and schools of tame tropical fish.

a barrier reef submerged in less than 10 feet (3 meters) of water, to a breathtaking drop-off that plummets to waters more than 200 feet (60 meters) deep. To say the least, the swarms of tropical fish within the crater are friendly. They are long accustomed to having divers drop in on them with fish food, so be prepared to be surrounded by swarms of small, curious, exotically painted fish, such as lemon butterflyfish, Moorish idols, and parrotfish, which will crowd around to be hand fed.

A wide variety of charter boats trek daily to Molokini (weather permitting), carrying sightseers and skin and scuba divers from Wailea, Kihei, Maalaea Bay, and Lahaina. Morning is the best time to experience Molokini as the water tends to be calmer; during the afternoon wind and waves pick up and things can get pretty rough.

Typical Depth Range:	10–30 feet (3–10 meters)
Typical Current Conditions:	Non-existent within the bay
Expertise Required:	Novice
Access:	Beach

Maui's nearby neighbor is Lanai, also known as the "Pineapple Island." The entire island is owned by the Dole Corporation, and the industry there, as might be expected, is pineapple growing. It is a rural island with a population of only 2,000. Lanai City has a small country-style inn; there are some rental vehicles and ground tours available for those who are interested.

Divers reach Lanai by boat from Maui; it is a day-long affair. Incoming vessels are no longer permitted to anchor in Hulopoe Bay itself, but must off-load passengers at nearby Manele Harbor. A few minutes' walk brings you to the idyllic South Seas beauty of Hulopoe Bay.

Like Molokini Crater, Hulope Bay on the south shore of Lanai is a marine park. Dive and snorkel tour boats make the run to Hulopoe Bay from Maui daily.

Snorkeling. Hulopoe is visited daily by large sailing and motor vessels. These generally allow only snorkeling, not scuba, and are planned more as family and group outings with a shoreside barbecue and open bar on the return trip.

The most interesting part of the bay is on the left-hand side. There is a wide reef ledge with large tide pools for interesting exploration and swimming. Just over this ledge is a shallow submerged reef teeming with schools of bright tropical fish, and turtles are occasionally seen leisurely finning by. It's an excellent spot for the novice snorkeler, since complete instruction is provided in the calm, bathtub-warm waters of Hulopoe.

Although dive boats come into Hulopoe, the main scuba itnerest at Lanai is the nearby Cathedrals.

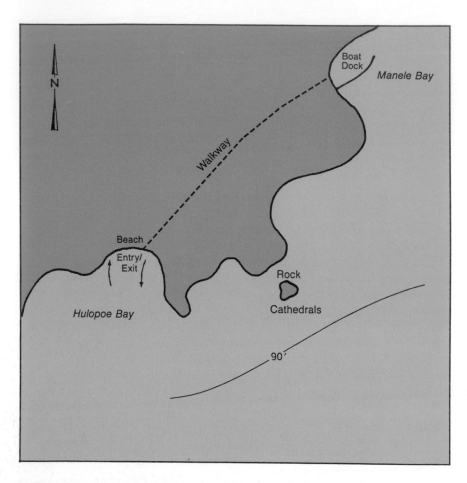

Hulopoe Bay and the Cathedrals on Lanai Island are reached by boat from Maui; it is a day-long trip, but it's worth the effort.

Lanai Island — The Cathedrals 3

Typical Depth Range: 70 feet (21 meters)
Typical Current Conditions: Mild to treacherous
Expertise Required: Advanced
Access: Boat

Offshore from Hulopoe Bay are two of Lanai's standout dive sites — the Cathedrals. Located within a few miles (less than 5 kilometers) of each other, the first and second Cathedrals are huge underwater grottos that form a series of lava arches, caverns, pinnacles, tubes, ridges, and interconnecting passageways. When the water is calm, the visibility is generally in excess of 100 feet (30 meters).

The Cathedrals off Lanai are large, dramatic underwater caves. Tortuous interconnecting lava tubes open into enormous caverns, dappled with sunlight streaming through crevices in the rocky ceiling.

When you enter the mammoth undersea grottos, you soon see how the Cathedrals got their names. Narrow passageways open into caves, which in turn open into vast cathedral-like chambers. Looking up, you see sunlight filtering in through holes in the rocky ceiling, producing fantastic light patterns that shimmer and dance laser-like in the darkened amphitheater. The sight is reminiscent of glass windows in a cathedral.

Unusual Marine Life. The area abounds in clouds of small tropical fish which seem to segregate themselves according to color. Many specimens of delicately painted butterflyfish thrive here, as do schools of Moorish idols. Within the nooks and crannies you can find lobsters, crabs, and other curious creatures.

Morning is the best time to dive the Cathedrals, when the wind and water swell is down. In the afternoon swift currents may develop unexpectedly, with tremendous water surges stirring up the bottom and reducing visibility to zero. **The Cathedrals should only be dived with experienced local divers.**

Schools of Moorish idols can be found in the recesses of the Cathedrals. Other tropical species abound, and eagle rays sometimes graze the sand channels between the cavern structures.

Typical Depth Range:	30–60 feet (10–20 meters)
Typical Current Conditions:	Mild
Expertise Required:	Novice
Access:	Boat

Nobody is quite sure why the turtles have picked this particular spot, but off Lanai's east coast there is a place that might best be described as "turtle city."

Whatever the reason for their proclivity for this rather restricted locale, if you want to see turtles — up close and lots of them — this is the place! In other dive sites around the Hawaiian Islands you may, on any given day, stand a fair chance of seeing a turtle or two. But at Lanai's turtle dive, you are almost guaranteed to see at least several of the large, friendly, graceful creatures on *every* dive. It's a unique diving experience.

Best diving conditions are in the morning before the afternoon winds come up. Visibility tends to be better earlier in the day and the water calmer. Also, when the winds come up it can be a rather uncomfortable ride back to Maui, as it can take an hour or more.

Bottom terrain at the turtle dive shows good topography. Large volcanic rock mounds, encrusted with corals, are surrounded by sand channels,

Lanai's turtle dive features sea turtles both large and small. Being quite accustomed to people, they are easily approached.

Besides turtles, the turtle dive site has an abundance of other interesting marine life, such as large octopi, which are seen on nearly every dive.

ravines cut through the rock, and, in general, very scenic surroundings. Even if there were no turtles, marine life is abundant and octopus are frequently sighted.

But it's the turtles that make this site so memorable. Being well-accustomed to people, sea turtles tamely swim right up to divers as if to welcome them to their watery home. By swimming slowly, exhaling gently, and not making any sudden movements to startle them, you can approach the turtles close enough to pet them. It is a photographer's paradise, and you can commonly expect to get at least 2 or 3 turtles in pictures as they glide about the divers.

Typical Depth Range:	10–40 feet (3–12 meters)
Typical Current Conditions:	Calm during summer months; rough to undiveable in the winter
Expertise Required:	Novice to intermediate
Access:	Beach

Located at the westernmost tip of Maui is Honolua Bay. Hololua and adjoining Makuleia Bay are found some 8 miles (13 kilometers) north of Kaanapali by following Route 30, the Honoapiilani Highway.

Marine Life. Both sides of the bay feature lovely, well-developed coral reefs in shallow water of 40 feet (12 meters) or less. Between these reefs, in the center of the bay, is a sandy bottom. The fish seen in the greatest numbers on the Hololua reefs are species of wrasse, primarily the saddleback variety with a blue head, a green tail, and a red midsection or "saddle." The Hawaiian name for these reef fish common to all Hawaiian waters, is "hinalea." Nature seems to have endowed these

Butterflyfish abound on Hawaii's luxuriant reefs. One of the larger species is the ornate butterflyfish, which often swims in pairs or small groups.

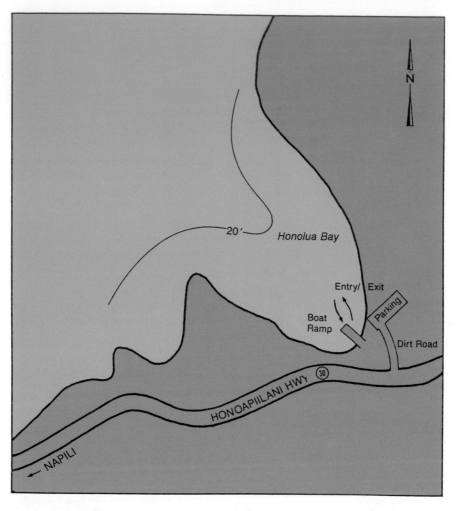

Lovely, well-developed coral reefs in shallow water can be found at Honolua Bay

finned creatures with an unusual sense of curiosity. They are well-known for following divers about and darting in close to peer into a face mask to see what the air-breathing intruder is up to.

There do not tend to be any large, spectacularly towering coral or rock formations, although there are a smattering of small caves along the left side of the bay. The coral growth is lush, however, and the marine life plentiful. Remember, Honolua Bay is a protected Marine Preserve, and the collection of shells, coral, and fish is strictly prohibited.

Geographically, Hololua Bay is on the tip of west Maui just before the beginning of the north shore. At the north shore of any of the Hawaiian islands, time of year and daily weather conditions are important factors to consider before attempting to dive. Diving is best during the summer months or whenever the water is flat. The best time of day is in the morning, before the wind and waves come up. Hololua Bay also has an international reputation among surfers who flock here to compete during the winter months when the big surf rolls in. **Do not attempt to dive the bay during such time!**

Honolua Bay, on the western tip of Maui, is another protected marine park. Two reefs, on the two sides of the bay, are separated by a flat sand bottom.

Black Rock 6

Typical Depth Range:	20 feet (6 meters) in cove area
Typical Current Conditions:	Nonexistent most of the year
Expertise Required:	Novice inside the sheltered cove; intermediate outside
Access:	Beach

Black Rock is probably the easiest, safest, and most convenient dive spot on Maui. It is located on Kaanapali beach, in front of the Sheraton Hotel. While the large expanse of Kaanapali beach consists only of sandy bottom terrain, a large black volcanic-rock peninsula juts out several hundred feet from shore, providing a protected cove that is excellent for the novice snorkeler and scuba enthusiast. The hotels in the area rent snorkel gear and underwater cameras; they also provide instruction.

The underwater terrain contains a little coral but mostly volcanic rock; an abundance of tame tropical fish can be found here. In places such as Black Rock and Molokini where divers drop into the water every day,

Kaanapali Beach, viewed from the top of the Sheraton Hotel, is the site of the Black Rock diving area. The best diving is found to the extreme right side of this photo.

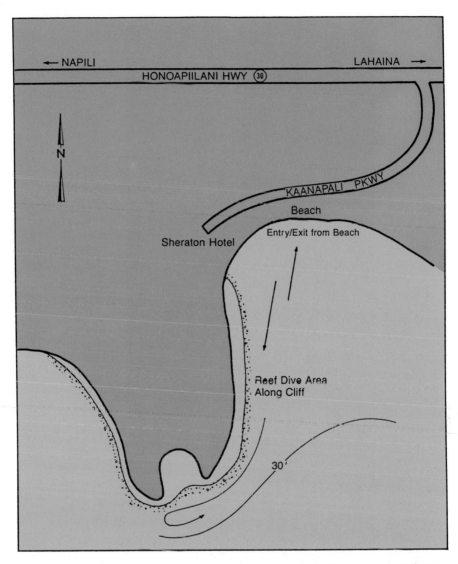

Black Rock is named after the black volcanic rock peninsula that forms a protected cove, perfect for both divers and snorkelers.

colorful reef fish, such as trumpetfish, lemon butterflyfish, parrotfish, and damselfish, have become extremely tame. They are used to being fed and swarm about scuba divers and snorkelers alike. Great for pictures!

The best entry is the beach adjoining the Black Rock peninsula. For the snorkeler who is not weighted down with cumbersome scuba gear,

Beginning divers and snorkelers find Black Rock made to order. Entry from shore is easy along the beach, and the dive site is very near in shallow, calm water.

entry can be made from the rock jetty itself, but watch out for ocean swells and waves. The sheltered inner cove is recommended for the novice skin and scuba divers. Those with more experience will find better visibility and more marine life by swimming out around the rocky peninsula to the north. Depending on daily conditions, there may be a bit of a current to contend with. The water tends to be clearer outside the cove, and the rocky shoreline provides for some good scenery and fish life.

Although Black Rock is not the best beach dive found in Maui in terms of scenic seascapes and abundance of coral and marine life, it does offer proximity, ease of diving, an excellent beach, and shoreside amenities and services. It may be the best spot for those who wish to get a taste of the excitement of the underwater world without going through the time, expense, and trouble of a long boat ride or a drive to more distant dive sites. Black Rock is also highly recommended for beginning night divers.

Typical Depth Range:	20–50 feet (6–15 meters)
Typical Current Conditions:	Mild
Expertise Required:	Novice
Access:	Boat

For an easy, fun dive that requires little time to reach, the Lahaina dive is highly recommended. The site is near shore (though a bit far for a comfortable beach dive) and in shallow, calm water. Depending on tide and surface conditions, visibility tends to be good — 50 feet plus even in shallow water.

The bottom terrain tends to be rather flat, with little topography. But scenic topography is not what's featured at this site. In addition to being a very easy dive, the abundant coral growth and fish life make this site very attractive. There are larger brain corals, finger corals, and branching antler coral gardens, which provide unlimited shelter for all kinds of fish.

The fish here are accustomed to divers visiting, and flock around once the boat has anchored and people begin entering the water. It's a great spot for both snorkeling and scuba diving. The water is shallow and clear enough so that snorkelers paddling on the surface can see the scuba divers exploring the reef not far below.

There are all kinds of fish here for the photography enthusiast. Schools of black triggerfish are friendly and very photogenic. Butterflyfish abound, both in schools or individually, congregating in and about the lush coral growth.

The Lahaina dive site offers shallow, calm, clear waters with lots of coral and fish. A great boat dive for beginners.

Typical Depth Range:	35 feet (11 meters) on the reefs
Typical Current Conditions:	Generally mild to nonexistent
Expertise Required:	Novice
Access:	Beach

Olowalu is one of the best sites for underwater scenery and marine life. Getting here does require a few more miles of driving, but the site is very accessible and an easily dived area for the beginner.

As you drive east out of Lahaina, you will come to the Olowalu General Store. Go about 1 mile (1½ kilometers) farther and you can dive nearly

A freckled hawkfish caught in a characteristic pose, perched atop a small coral bush.

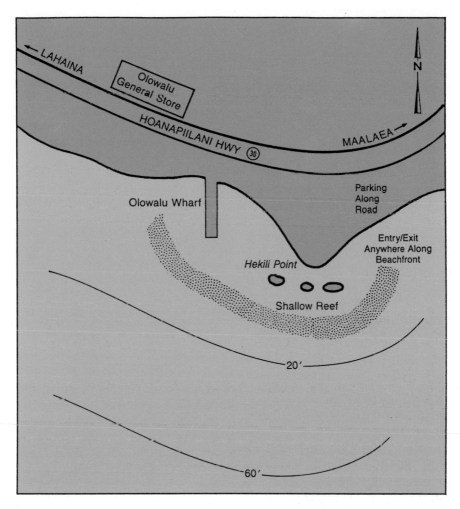

When the surf is down, Olowalu is an excellent spot for underwater photography, and great for snorkeling.

anywhere along the beachfront. There is a long stretch of sandy beach for easy entry and exit. However, there are few shade trees at Olowalu, so things can get pretty hot.

When the surf is up, this area is not good for diving. The coral is shallow and dangerous when the water is rough, and if you see surfers out on the water, you can assume that the good surfing conditions make it a poor time for diving, so try another spot for safety's sake.

When the surf is down, however, there is a lot to see. This area features good coral-reef development, and it is a good place for underwater photo-

Easy entry, plentiful marine life, and shallow water make Olowalu a good choice for snorkelers and divers willing to drive a bit out of the way.

graphy — you can see an abundance of reef life. Nearer to shore, the water is rather shallow and recommended for snorkeling. It's really too shallow for scuba, and those with tanks should swim further out to deeper water. Although you will not see such spectacular underwater terrain as dramatic coral heads and lava tubes that you might see at some other sites, this is an excellent spot for easily accessible reef diving by the neophyte snorkeler and scuba diver.

Wailea Beach 9

Typical Depth Range:	55 feet (17 meters)
Typical Current Conditions:	Mild to nonexistent most of the year
Expertise Required:	Novice near shore; intermediate farther out
Access:	Beach

Wailea Beach and the offshore reef extending south to Polo Beach offer some of East Maui's easiest and nicest skin and scuba diving. To find the beach, travel toward Makena, past the Intercontinental Hotel and Wailea Shopping Village on your right, until you see the sign indicating Wailea Beach. There is a paved parking lot and you must walk a short

When alarmed or threatened, the porcupine pufferfish swallows water, thus expanding its girth, causing its protective spines to stick straight out.

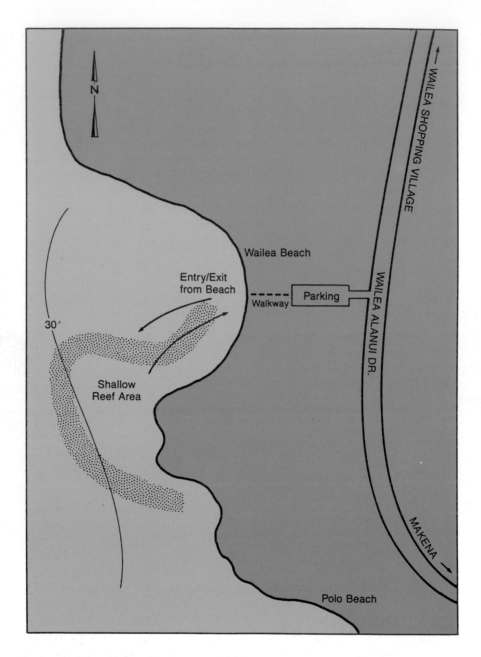

The best diving at Wailea Beach is along the lava rock outcropping, which sticks straight out from shore.

Potter's angelfish is one of the more brilliantly colored fish found in Hawaiian waters.

distance down to the water. Sticking straight out from the shore is a large outcropping of lava rock that makes the best entry and exit point.

The best diving sites are also out along this lava rock outcropping. The reef extends around the coastline, and you can follow it all the way to Polo Beach if you're a hardy swimmer. Keep in mind that skin and scuba divers not venturing too far from Wailea Beach need only have beginning abilities, while swimming farther out requires intermediate skills.

The reef is quite extensive, with some very nice scenery, though without the abundance of fish life you will see elsewhere. The farther out you go and the deeper the water, the more you can expect to see. If you plan to swim from Wailea to Polo Beach to see all the sights along the way, it is recommended that you have someone drive the car to meet you at Polo Beach — the last before you get to Makena. Only attempt this swim if you are in good shape!

Typical Depth Range:	45 feet (14 meters)
Typical Current Conditions:	Generally mild to nonexistent
Expertise Required:	Intermediate
Access:	Beach

Just as Maui is described as "no ka oi" (the best), Makena is certainly "no ka oi" on this side of the island. Makena is about 3 miles (5 kilometers) past Polo Beach along the Makena Road.

There are two dive spots on the right-hand side of the long crescent of Makena Beach. The rocky coastline peninsula just to the right of the beach is the closest and easiest place to dive. Swim to the right out along this peninsula to find the best skin and scuba diving.

Schools of spotted lemon butterflyfish are common in Hawaiian waters. They are a schooling variety, and, in areas frequented by people, are very tame and friendly.

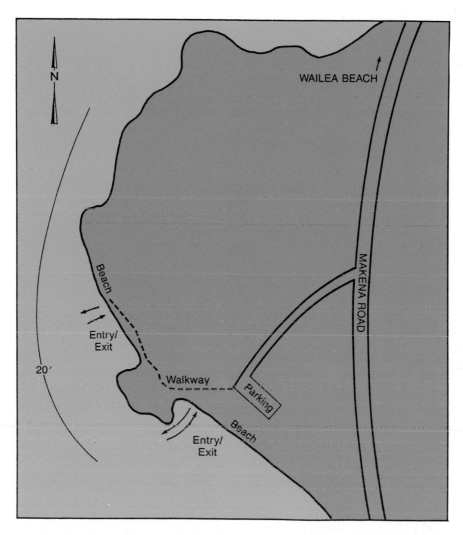

The underwater terrain at Makena Beach features good topographic relief, caves, and an abundance of fish and other marine life.

The best diving at Makena requires a bit of a walk to the small beach, but once there you'll find probably the finest beach-access skin and scuba diving on this side of the island. The choicest spots are found by swimming out from the right side of this beach along the coastline. The underwater terrain features good topographic relief, caves, and an abundance of fish, including various species of butterflyfish, and other marine life, like colorful crabs.

5

Diving the Big Island of Hawaii

The Kona Coast of Hawaii offers what many people feel is the best diving in the state. Maui's underwater enthusiasts may disagree, but only to an extent — Kona has some great diving! The southernmost island, Hawaii possesses the most extensive and well-developed coral reefs. The island has 3 long coastlines, but due to water conditions only the leeward Kona side is regularly dived. The waters on the Hilo side, because they face directly into the breath of the tradewinds, should not be dived except with a dive-shop guide who knows the local waters. Dive sites are fairly inaccessible from shore; most require boat access and you have to know the right places to go at the right time for comfortable, safe diving. Some spots, such as Waipio Bay, are so scenic abovewater that you figure they must be terrific underwater as well; unfortunately this is not always the case. If you want to dive the Hilo side, check with a dive shop.

The Kona coast is certainly the easiest side of the island to dive. Local divers, in fact, say it's hard to find a bad spot anywhere from Mahukona to South Point.

Sandy beaches and bays that indent the coastline show Hawaii's tropical charm.

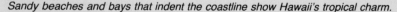

Dive Site Ratings

	Novice Diver	Novice Diver with Instructor or Divemaster	Intermediate Diver	Intermediate Diver with Instructor or Divemaster	Advanced Diver	Advanced Diver with Instructor or Divemaster
Hawaii						
1 Puako			x	x	x	x
2 Kona Surf Hotel	x	x	x	x	x	x
3 Honaunau Bay*	x	x	x	x	x	x
4 Red Hill	x	x	x	x	x	x
5 Kealakekua Bay*	x	x	x	x	x	x

* Indicates good snorkeling spot

When using this chart, see the information on pages 1-2 for an explanation of the diver rating system and site locations.

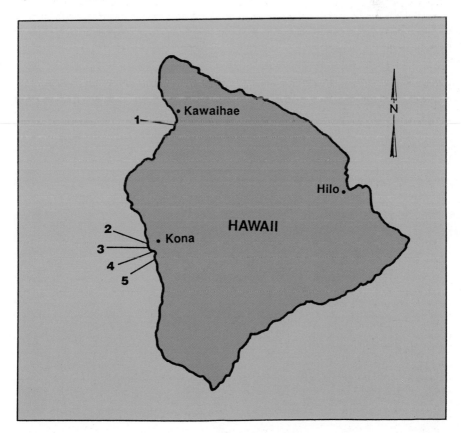

The long Kona Coast of the Big Island offers fine diving in the lee of the prevailing tradewinds.

Typical Depth Range:	20–90 feet (6–30 meters)
Typical Current Conditions:	Negligible much of the year, but the surf can be unpredictable for shore dives
Expertise Required:	Novice to intermediate for boat dives; intermediate to advanced for shore dives
Access:	Beach or boat

Puako offers many boat dive sites along this area of coastline; beach entries can be made along the 2-mile (3-kilometer) Puako Beach Road just off Highway 19, some 25 miles (40 kilometers) north of Kona.

Benefitting from the Big Island's position at the southernmost edge of the Hawaiian chain, coral development is the best in the state. Orange corals like this are found in abundance on the near shore reefs.

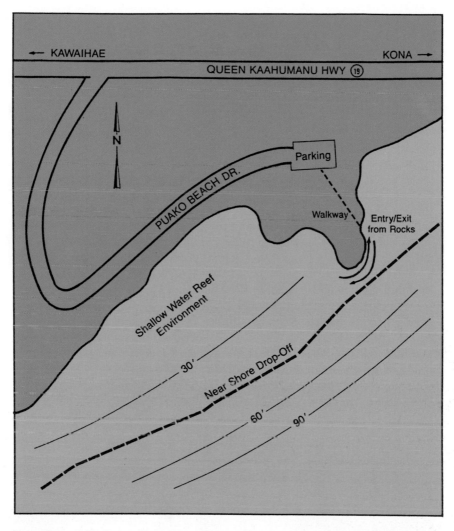

KAWAIHAE ←

KONA →

QUEEN KAAHUMANU HWY (19)

N

PUAKO BEACH DR.

Parking

Walkway

Entry/Exit
from Rocks

Shallow Water Reef
Environment

30'

Near Shore Drop-Off

60'

90'

Shore diving at Puako is well worth the effort, once you've made it across the sharp, volcanic rocks on the beach.

A word of caution about shore diving: there is no beach, only sharp volcanic rock that you must cross to reach the water. Wear tennis shoes, or at least sandals, to save your feet. The waveswept rocks are also very slippery and dangerous. But perhaps the worst thing about shore diving Puako is the surf — it can be glassy when you submerge, yet very rough when you surface again, making exiting hazardous. The best, calmest time to dive is morning. Almost assuredly, the surf will be up in the afternoon.

Shore diving at Puako is well worth the effort once you're in the water. The reef edge drops to depths of about 15–20 feet (5–6 meters), gradually sloping out to 60–90 feet (18–30 meters) at the drop-off further offshore. The shoreline is cut by surge channels, which produce fantastic topography including arch-like canyons, lava tubes, tunnels, walls, caverns, and the like. Within a few hundred feet of shore, towering coral reef formations take over, with valleys and rises 20–30 feet (6–10 meters) high, a splendid seascape with endless terrain to explore. Schools of tropical fish — lemon butterfly fish, parrotfish, and Moorish idols, for example — abound. Turtles are frequently sighted, and you may come upon them resting in the larger grottos. During the season, whales are often seen playing in the calm waters near shore.

If you like to dive on your own, Puako is a good spot if you keep in mind the rigors of shore entry and exit and the skill level reuired to dive safely. You can even stay at the nearby Puako Beach Apartments. You'll need a car to get to a local dive shop in order to get your tanks filled.

Guided Tours. The best dive sites between Puako and Mahukona are most conveniently reached by boat.

The coastline farther north is similar to Puako, and boats anchor in sheltered areas with good visibility, excellent underwater topography, and lots of marine life. The entire area is great for underwater photography. Numerous dive sites in the Mahukona vicinity feature caves and tunnels that penetrate back under the shoreline, with lobster seen on most dives.

Many excellent scuba diving and snorkeling sites can be found within swimming distance of the islands' golden beaches.

Typical Depth Range:	15–30 feet (5–10 meters)
Typical Current Conditions:	Generally negligible most of the year
Expertise Required:	Novice
Access:	Beach or boat

The Kona Surf Hotel is located just south of Keauhou Bay, opposite a most interesting dive area.

The Manta Ray Night Dive. Local dive shops and dive tour companies also offer boat dives to this site, and this very interesting night-dive package was started some years ago. It's called the manta ray night dive and, obviously, manta rays frequent this area. The Kona Surf is one of the largest hotels on the bay and shines powerful lights out onto the water that attract the great mantas if conditions, especially the weather, are right. The mantas follow their food source, microscopic plankton, which only come near the surface when there is little or no moon.

Kaiwa. There is, of course, no guarantee that the manta rays will be seen on any given dive. If they do not come around, this dive site is not

The masked butter-flyfish is another colorful, commonly seen reef inhabitant. They are not usually a schooling variety and more often travel about individually or in small groups.

Small reef white-tip sharks are sometimes seen on Hawaii's near-shore reefs. They will sometimes be encountered on the sand bottom under a ledge.

particularly good as far as bottom terrain and marine life are concerned, and an alternate site will be chosen by the tour operator. Often this alternate will be the south side of Kaiwa, a lovely spot for both day and night dives, though it can only be reached by boat. The area abounds in invertebrates, lobsters, and sleeping parrotfish in a nice coral garden. In closer to shore the bottom is shallow, about 20 feet (6 meters), with interesting arches and caves and a shark cave that often contains reef white-tip sharks. About 40 yards (37 meters) from shore the depth is 45 feet (12 meters), and then there is suddenly a dramatic drop-off that goes straight down into deep, open ocean water. The area is full of fish and is excellent for photography.

Typical Depth Range:	15–75 feet (5–23 meters)
Typical Current Conditions:	Not a factor unless there is a south swell
Expertise Required:	Novice to advanced
Access:	Beach

Historic Honaunau, also known as the City of Refuge, is so named because it served in ancient Hawaiian times as a sanctuary for criminals and warriors defeated in battle.

Honaunau Bay is a good spot for beach diving with good near-shore scenery. Drive past the restrooms and picnic area and park near the sandy

Honaunau Bay is a good spot for beach diving, but check local weather conditions to be certain the surf is down, and watch out for sea urchins!

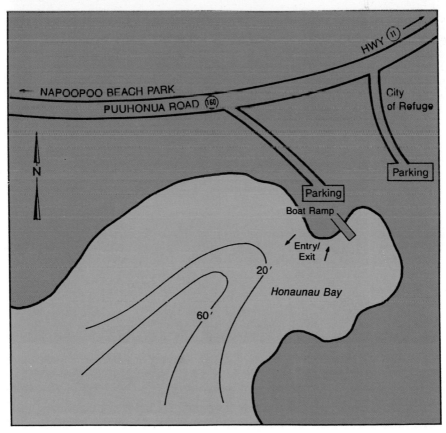

Honaunau Bay is excellent for scuba divers and snorkelers of all skill levels. Shallow, calm waters and nice reef development make it a favored site for easy underwater exploration.

beach, where you can cross a low lava-rock shelf for the best entry into the water. Two notes of caution here: check local weather conditions to be certain the surf is down, and watch out for the sea urchins. Rubber booties or shoes are recommended for getting into and exiting the water.

In Honaunau Bay itself, the bottom drops off fairly quickly. The shoreline is rugged, with arches and canyons that cut back into the shore that are interesting to explore.

If you swim farther out into the bay, there is a steep ledge that drops off to about 150 feet (45 meters). The bay abounds with fish life. Typically, you can see goatfish, parrotfish, and butterflyfish.

Honaunau Bay is a bit distant from Kona and thus not frequented by dive tours. Because it offers shore entry, it is recommended for those who wish to dive on their own rather than with an organized group. Before making the drive, check weather conditions with a local dive shop to be sure there is not south swell that could make diving dangerous. The skill level here ranges from novice to advanced, depending on whether you stay close to shore or venture further out into deeper water. Plan your dive according to your level of experience.

Parrotfish are so named because of their parrot-like beak and coloration. These fish are essential to reef development since, with their tough beaks, they scrape algae off the coral. Left alone, the algae would overgrow and kill the coral colonies.

Red Hill 4

Typical Depth Range:	15–75 feet (5–23 meters)
Typical Current Conditions:	Not a factor unless there is a south swell
Expertise Required:	Novice to advanced
Access:	Boat

Red Hill lies some 8 miles south of Kona, several hundred yards offshore. It is named after a distinctive, half cinder-cone that is now an extinct, submerged crater. The dive area is actually a large bay approximately ½ mile (1 kilometer) across.

Red Hill is one of the more popular dive sites in the Kona area. It is frequented daily by local divers and dive shop tours. Everybody has a favorite spot and almost anywhere is good. The cinder-cone crater is honeycombed with a series of remarkable shallow-water lava tubes. Some of these are as much as 10 feet (3 meters) in diameter; many are illuminated along their entire length by shafts of sunlight shining through holes in the roof. The lava tubes average about 50 feet (15 meters) deep; some are open at both ends while others are dead ends. Outside the lava tubes are other lava rock formations offering varied scenery: canyon ways, surge channels, pits, walls, ledges, drop-offs, and overhangs.

Fantasy Reef and Driftwood. Two areas within Red Hill are of particular note — Fantasy Reef and Driftwood, lying about 400–500 yards (370–462 meters) apart. Fantasy Reef has been linked to a fantasy land of undulating coral and lava-rock hills, with yellow and green plating corals, elkhorn and pink corals, and hovering schools of delicately painted butterflyfish, Moorish idols, and curious bluehead wrasse. The main feature of Fantasy Reef is its labyrinthine network of canyons. These canyons may be only 6 feet (2 meters) across on top of the reef and descend 20 or 25 feet (6–8 meters) down into the rock. Like a maze, these canyons frequently branch off into other channels. It is really a remarkable place to explore. Although this area is not really dangerous or difficult to dive, the diver does need to keep careful track of directions, and not wander too far away from the boat.

Driftwood does not have the spectacular terrain that Fantasy Reef does, but the topography is quite interesting. It is actually an underwater peninsula that sticks out from shore and contains cave complexes. One of these is a shark cave where you have a 50/50 chance of coming across its resident small white-tip sharks.

Red Hill is best done as a two-tank dive; Fantasy Reef one dive, Driftwood the second.

Typical Depth Range:	20–90 feet (6–28 meters)
Typical Current Conditions:	Generally nonexistent most of the year
Expertise Required:	Novice
Access:	Beach or boat

Kealakekua Bay is another spot of historic significance. Capt. James Cook, the discoverer of the Hawaiian Islands, was killed here in a battle with local islanders in 1779.

Abovewater, Kealakckua Bay offers a spectacular panorama of sheer, majestic volcanic cliffs honeycombed with ancient Hawaiian burial caves. On the other side of the bay is the quietly rural Hawaiian village of Napoopoo, where the islanders still fish just as their ancestors did.

Unusual Marine Life. Kealakekua Bay is a protected underwater park, which means that nothing except pictures and memories can be taken out of the water. As a result, the 315-acre bay abounds with schools of tame tropical fish, which are accustomed to being fed by visiting divers. Many other types of marine life prefer the sheltered waters of the bay, such as

Convict tangs, named for their black-and-white striped coloration, are just one of the tame species to be found in the underwater park at Kealakekua.

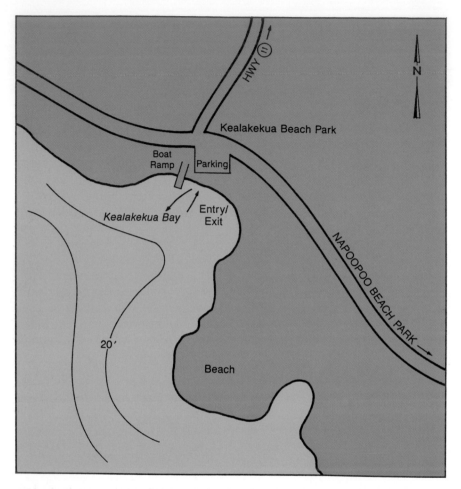

Kealakekua Bay is a protected underwater park; as a result, the bay abounds with tame tropical fish, accustomed to being fed by divers.

Captain James Cook

When visiting Hawaii in 1779, Captain James Cook, English navigator and explorer, and his men were at first held in awe by the native Islanders, who were amazed by their fair skin, strange new customs, and the fact that the Englishmen had come from so far away. But Cook and his men broke local traditions and taboos, angering the Hawaiians. A fight broke out over a stolen boat, and Cook was killed. His men fled the Islands.

A diver cradles an inflated pufferfish in the marine park at Kealakekua Bay. The fish swallows water as a defense mechanism against predators; however, this also renders them immovable and easy prey to playful divers.

spotted eagle rays, gorgeously tinted nudibranchs, curious wrasse, butterflyfish, reclusive moray eels, and lots of coral. Kealakekua Bay is a popular place to bring visiting divers because of its sheltered waters, friendly fish, and beautiful underwater terrain.

If you are going to explore Kealakekua Bay on your own, the best water entry is on the Napoopoo side. There is a small beach park and shade trees where you can park. The clear water offers good skin and scuba diving quite close to shore for the novice. For the more hardy and experienced diver, a longer swim further out into the bay reveals rolling coral hills, clearer and deeper water, and even more fish life.

A number of dive-tour boats bring visitors to Kealakekua Bay every day. Fish immediately flock to arriving boats and greet divers as they enter the water, hoping for a handout of fish food. Kealakekua Bay is one of the nicest, easiest, and most conveniently dived spots on the Kona coast.

6

Diving Kauai

Lying approximately 21 degrees north of the equator, the Hawaiian Islands are at the fringe of the warm water coral belt. Since Kauai is the northernmost island in the chain, corals flourish less in its water than around the isles further south. Nonetheless, Kauai has an abundance of dive sites and some first-rate diving facilities. There are dive shops and dive-tour companies in Kapaa, Hanalei, and Poipu.

The north shore, of course, catches more weather. It does have some excellent sites, but due to the sometimes quickly varying moods of wind and water, it is best to go with a dive tour to dive safely. The island's best, easiest, nearly year-round dive sites are found on the leeward southern shore. The beaches of Poipu are gorgeous and here you will find the greatest variety of hotels and condos, as well as a plethora of dive shops, as well as skin- and scuba-tour and equipment-rental outfits.

Kauai is very lush, and is noted for its tropical forests and waterfalls. Sightseeing is a popular pastime for visitors and residents alike.

Dive Site Ratings

	Novice Diver	Novice Diver with Instructor or Divemaster	Intermediate Diver	Intermediate Diver with Instructor or Divemaster	Advanced Diver	Advanced Diver with Instructor or Divemaster
Kauai						
1 Ke'e Lagoon*	x	x	x	x	x	x
2 Haena	x	x	x	x	x	x
3 Ahukini*			x	x	x	x
4 Koloa Landing	x	x	x	x	x	x
5 Poipu Beach	x	x	x	x	x	x

* Indicates good snorkeling spot

When using this chart, see the information on pages 1-2 for an explanation of the diver rating system and site locations.

Kauai is the place residents of the other islands go to get away. Although the northernmost island in the chain (and thus less coral development), Kauai offers some fine dive sites and a relaxed, noncommercial atmosphere.

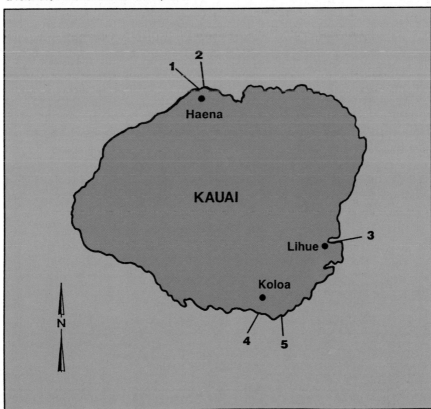

Typical Depth Range:	10–20 feet (3–6 meters)
Typical Current Conditions:	Steady current most of the year along the left side of the beach; can be dangerous when strong. Much calmer to the right side of lagoon
Expertise Required:	Novice to intermediate
Access:	Beach

To begin with, remember that the north shore of Kauai, like the north shore of all islands, is calmest and safest during the summer months. Winter brings large surf and dangerous water conditions.

Scenic Ke'e Lagoon is found just to the west of Haena Beach Park. The lagoon itself is really too shallow for good scuba diving and is recommended for snorkelers or very novice scuba divers just getting used to the ocean. Depending on your level of experience, swim either to the left or the right; the right side is best for beginners, with a maximum depth of around 12 feet (4 meters). It is also calmer here. The terrain forms a channel as you swim to the right, running some distance along the shore. There are some interesting little ledges and fish life in this area.

To the left of the lagoon, within 50–70 yards (45–63 meters) of shore, the water gets down to 20 feet (6 meters) in depth. This area is recommended for the intermediate or advanced diver because of the presence of mild to strong currents. There are some nice ledges here and more abundant fish life than to the right side of the lagoon.

The visibility in the lagoon is generally good, about 40–60 feet (12–18 meters), weather-dependent of course. The area is frequented by large schools of striped convict tangs known locally as "manini." The bay is almost a fish nursery, and many juvenile species are seen there.

If the water is calm — and only if the water is calm — you can swim past the inner lagoon to the outer reef, where the diving is lovely. Depth averages 10–40 feet (3–12 meters); there are caves, great visibility, and a lot to see.

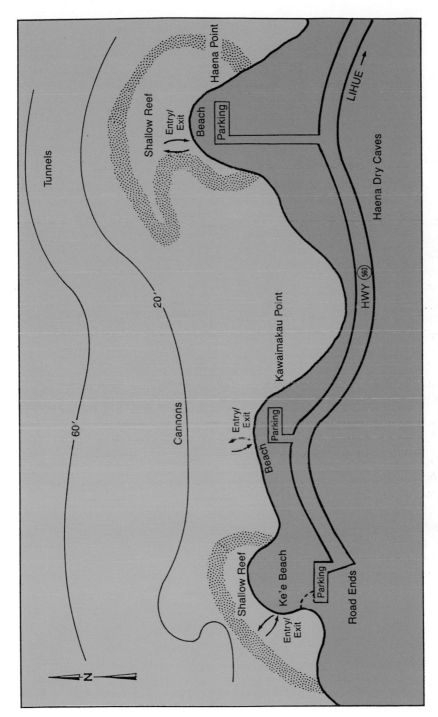

Novice to intermediate divers will enjoy diving at Keʼe Lagoon and Tunnels and Cannons reefs at Haena.

Inside the reef at Ke'e Lagoon, snorkelers find a varied seascape in shallow water. Outside the reef, the deeper water affords excellent visibility, with many caves and ledges to explore.

92

Haena 2

Typical Depth Range:	5–65 feet (2–20 meters)
Typical Current Conditions:	Mild to strong at 20 feet (6 meters) or more
Expertise Required:	Novice to intermediate
Access:	Beach

There are actually 2 dive sites at Haena: Cannon's Reef and Tunnels Reef, as they are known locally.

Entry to Cannon's Reef is best made through the V-shaped slit in the reef, which also makes a good exit point. It is 5–10 feet (2–3 meters)

Bigeyes derive their name for an obvious reason. They can be found hiding in the shelter of crevices and caves at Haena Beach.

A shallow bowl — a sandy bottom surrounded by reef — is one of the features of the Tunnels site in Haena Bay. Farther out, ledges, caves, and overhangs can be found. Lizardfish are often seen on the sand bottom. Photo: B. Sastre.

deep here. As you follow the ledge, the water gets rapidly deeper, ultimately reaching 70 feet (21 meters) deep.

The most extensive and more popular reef is Tunnels. The most convenient parking place is actually about ¼ mile (½ kilometer) to the right, or east, of Haena. Here you will find a dirt road running down to the water and a boat channel. Novice divers should swim to the right, where the channel fans out into a large sandy-bottom pool surrounded by reef. The depth is about 7 feet (2 meters). From here you can swim further out as the sand bottom slopes gradually to a maximum depth of 25 feet (8 meters). There are some nice coral heads, caves, and fish here.

The experienced diver should head out to the left of the channel. Here the sandy bottom slopes down to 65 feet (20 meters). Bear in mind that the deeper you go, the more pronounced the current becomes. There are some particularly nice ledges, caves, and overhangs in the 50 foot (15 meter) range. White-tip reef sharks are frequently sighted here.

Typical Depth Range:	15–45 feet (5–14 meters)
Typical Current Conditions:	Very rough and dangerous most of the year; safe to dive during Kona weather
Expertise Required:	Intermediate
Access:	Beach

One of the choicest of Kauai's dive sites is found on the windward side of the island, past the Lihue airport at the end of Ahukini Road (the road ends at Hanamaula Bay).

Nudibranchs, similar to this one perched on a diver's finger, are often seen at Ahukini. Note the "gills" that extend from the creature's back for respiration. Photo: B. Sastre.

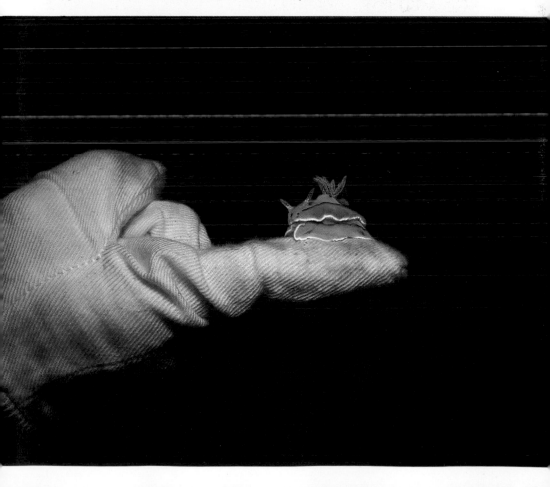

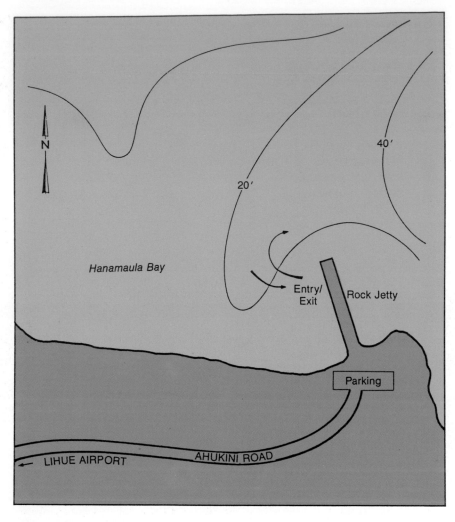

Varied marine life, such as lobster, crabs, fish, and nudibranchs, are found at Ahukini, but only dive on days when the southerly Kona winds are blowing.

Unfortunately, most of the year this area is undiveable due to north-west tradewinds that hit the coastline with pounding surf. On those few days out of the year when the southerly Kona winds are blowing, this area becomes calm and the diving is excellent.

The dive site is past a large rock jetty on the far right side of the bay. This jetty served as the pier for the old harbor before the new one was built at Nawiliwili. Entry can be made, if the water is really calm, directly over the rocks in front of the pier.

The disc butterflyfish is just one of the graceful, colorful tropical species that draws divers to Hawaii.

Once out to the dive site, the visibility is almost always good, 60–80 feet (18–25 meters) and more. There is a wide variety of reef shapes for interesting topography and exploration. The marine life is equally varied — lobster and crabs, butterflyfish, parrotfish, nudibranchs, and lots more. This is also a fairly regular stopping-off place for the humpback whale during the winter migrations, and divers have actually been able to touch these gentle giants during dives. When the weather is right, it's a great spot!

Typical Depth Range:	10–40 feet (3–12 meters)
Typical Current Conditions:	None
Expertise Required:	Novice to intermediate
Access:	Beach

Halfway between Koloa and Poipu Beach is a sheltered cove that is excellent for diving. This is Koloa Landing. A popular boat landing, Koloa is perhaps the favorite dive site on Kauai's south shore. It is a well-protected cove and, even when all other parts of the island are undiveable due to poor weather, this site is almost always calm. The cove features a large variety of coral, and the fish here are quite used to divers dropping in on them and are thus very tame, easily hand-fed, and very photogenic. The most common of these friendly finned creatures is the attractive blue-spotted snapper, which has an affinity for being hand-fed. Curious saddleback are also abundant.

There are two dive sites within the cove, to the right and to the left. The left side is a bit more barren, but it does have some nice coral and fish, although it is not nearly as attractive as the right side. The right side is the most popular among local divers and dive tours. In addition to many kinds of fish and interesting coral formations, it features some very tame moray eels, which frequently greet divers and are so accustomed to humans that they, too, can be hand-fed!

Photogenic fish, such as this saddleback wrasse, are accustomed to being fed at Koloa Landing.

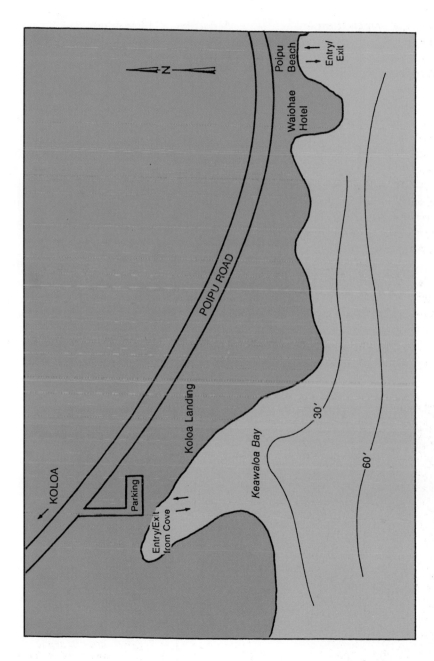

Because of its location in a well-protected cove, Koloa is perhaps the overall favorite dive on Kauai's south shore, while Poipu Beach is probably the best spot for the beginning snorkeler and scuba diver.

Typical Depth Range:	5–40 feet (2–12 meters)
Typical Current Conditions:	Not a factor in the cove; mild currents may exist outside the cove
Expertise Required:	Novice to intermediate
Access:	Beach

Poipu Beach Park is east of Koloa Landing, adjacent to the Waiohai Hotel. Poipu Beach is probably the best spot on the island of Kauai for the beginning snorkeler and scuba diver; novices can enjoy the underwater world in complete safety and comfort here. There is rarely any kind of current in the cove itself. Even on the outside, only mild currents are usually encountered.

There are a number of tide pools on one side of the cove. To the left of these pools the water is only 3–5 feet (1–2 meters) deep, and this is a good place for beginners to get their feet wet. From here you can swim out until the water becomes 10–20 feet (3–6 meters) deep; outside the cove depths average 30–40 feet (10–12 meters). The cove is frequented daily by dive shops and skin-diving tour companies. Thus the fish here are very accustomed to visitors and have become extremely tame and are easily hand-fed.

Huge schools of lemon-yellow butterflyfish often flock around near shore reefs. They are one of the most photogenic sights in Hawaii.

7

Safety

This section discusses common hazards, including dangerous marine animals, and emergency procedures in case of a diving accident. We do not discuss the diagnosis or treatment of serious medical problems; refer to your first aid manual or emergency diving accident manual for that information.

Diving Accidents

The Divers Alert Network (DAN), a membership association of individuals and organizations sharing a common interest in diving safety, operates a **24-hour national hotline (919) 684-8111** (collect calls are accepted in an emergency). DAN does not directly provide medical care; however, they do provide advice on early treatment, evacuation, and hyperbaric treatment of diving-related injuries. Additionally, DAN provides diving safety information to members to help prevent accidents. Membership is $10 a year, offering: the DAN *Underwater Diving Accident Manual,* describing symptoms and first aid for the major diving-related injuries and emergency room physician guidelines for drugs and i.v. fluids; a membership card listing diving-related symptoms on one side and DAN's emergency and non-emergency phone numbers on the other; 1 tank decal and 3 small equipment decals with DAN's logo and emergency number; and a newsletter, "Alert Diver," which describes diving medicine and safety information in layman's language, with articles for professionals, case histories, and medical questions related to diving. Special memberships for dive stores, dive clubs, and corporations are also available. The DAN Manual can be purchased for $4 from the Administrative Coordinator, National Diving Alert Network, Duke University Medical Center, Box 3823, Durham, NC 27710.

DAN divides the U.S. into 7 regions, each coordinated by a specialist in diving medicine who has access to the hyperbaric chambers in his region. Non-emergency or information calls are connected to the DAN office and information number, (919) 684-2948. This nsumber can be

Emergency Services

OAHU

Hospitals:
Queen's Medical Center
1301 Punchbowl
538-9011

Diving Doctors:
Call U.S. Navy Hyperbaric
facility at Submarine Base,
Pearl Harbor
422-5955

Recompression Facilities:
Submarine Base, Pearl Harbor
422-5955

Police:
911

MAUI

Hospitals:
Maui Memorial
221 Mahalani St.
Wailuku, Maui
244-9056

Diving Doctors:
Steven Strong
Kaiser Medical Clinic
502 Pavoa Rd.
Lahaina
661-0081

Recompression Facilities:
Maui Memorial
244-9056

Police:
911

BIG ISLAND

Hospitals:
Hilo Hospital
1190 Waianuenue Ave.
961-4211

Diving Doctors:
Contact Coast Guard
536-4336

Recompression Facilities:
Call Coast Guard for evacuation
to Honolulu, Pearl Harbor
536-4336

Police:
935-3311, Hilo
323-2645, Kona

KAUAI

Hospitals:
G.N. Wilcox Memorial Hospital
3420 Kuhio Hwy.
245-4811

Diving Doctors:
U.S. Navy Hyperbaric Facility
Pearl Harbor, Honolulu
422-5955

Recompression Facilities:
Call Coast Guard for evacuation
to Honolulu, Pearl Harbor
536-4336

Police:
911

dialed direct between 9 a.m. and 5 p.m. Monday–Friday Eastern Standard time. Divers should *not* call DAN for chamber locations. Chamber status changes frequently, making this kind of information dangerous if obsolete at the time of an emergency. Instead, divers should contact DAN as soon as a diving emergency is suspected. All divers should have comprehensive medical insurance and check to make sure that hyperbaric treatment and air ambulance services are covered internationally.

Diving is a safe sport and there are very few accidents compared to the number of divers and number of dives made each year. But when the infrequent injury does occur, DAN is ready to help. DAN, originally 100% federally funded, is now largely supported by the diving public. Membership in DAN or purchase of DAN manuals or decals provides divers with useful safety information and provides DAN with necessary operating funds. Donations to DAN are a deductible as DAN is a legal non-profit public service organization.

Dangerous Marine Animals

Sea Urchins. As in the rest of the world, the most common hazardous animal that divers will encounter in the Hawaiian Islands is the long-spined sea urchin. This urchin has spines that can penetrate wetsuits, booties, and gloves. Injuries are nearly always immediately painful, and sometimes infective. Urchins are found at every diving depth, although they are more common in shallow water near shore, especially under coral heads. At night the urchins come out of their hiding places and are even easier to bump into. Minor injuries can be treated by extracting the spines (it's worth a try, though they're hard to get out) and treating the wound with an antibiotic cream — make sure your tetanus immunization is current. Usually, spine bits fester and pop out several weeks later. Some people feel that crushing an embedded spine will make it dissolve faster in the tissues. Serious punctures will require a doctor's attention.

Barracudas. Barracudas are not commonly seen in Hawaiian waters, and are included in this section only because of their undeserved reputation for ferocity. If you do see barracudas, they will often get close enough to be at the edge of visibility.

Sting Rays. Sting rays can be seen in sand flats. They do not attack, but they don't like being sat on, stepped on, or prodded. They often are partially covered with sand, so look before you settle down on sandy bottoms. The long barbed stinger at the base of the tail can inflict a serious wound. Wounds are always extremely painful, often deep and infective, and can cause serious symptoms including anaphylactic shock.

If you get stung, head for the hospital and let a doctor take care of the wound.

Scorpionfish. Scorpionfish are well camouflaged, usually less than a foot (30 centimeters) long, and have poisonous spines hidden among their fins. They are often difficult to spot because they typically sit quietly on the bottom, looking more like plant-covered rocks than live fish. As with sting rays, watch where you put your hands and knees and you're not likely to meet one the hard way. If you get stung, severe allergic reactions are quite possible and great pain and infection are possible depending on the species. Head for the hospital and see a doctor.

Lionfish. Lionfish are in the same family as scorpionfish, but instead of lying camouflaged on the bottom, these fish can be seen quietly drifting along the reef, usually at night. They should not be touched as their sting can be quite serious.

Sharks. The most common sharks seen on the Hawaiian reefs are the sandbar shark, the black tip, and the Galapagos shark. The sandbar shark usually flees when it sees a diver, the other two are more curious. Often they swim close to investigate divers and then swim away. When any shark begins to hang around, it is best to leave the water.

Eels. Moray eels are dangerous only if harassed. There are lots of morays under coral heads and in crevices, and cornered eels will bite. Feeding and fondling morays is not recommended. If you get nipped, bites are sometimes infective and very painful and call for a doctor's attention.

The beautiful lionfish is graceful but deadly. The feather-like spines on its back can be used to inject a powerful venom.

Appendix

Dive Shops

The list below is included as a service to the reader. The author has made every effort to make this list complete at the time the book was printed. This list does not necessarily constitute an endorsement of these operators and dive shops. If operators/owners wish to be considered for inclusion in future reprints/editions, please contact Pisces Books, P.O. Box 2608, Houston, TX 77252-2608.

Oahu

Aaron's Dive Shop
46-215 Kahuhipa St.
Kaneohe, HI 96744
235-3877

Aaron's Dive Shop
602 Kailua Rd.
Kailua, HI 96734
261-1211

Aloha Dive Shop
Koko Marina Center
Honolulu, HI 96825
395-8882

Bojac Aquatic Center
94-801 Farrington Hwy.
Waipahu, HI 96797
671-0311

Breeze Hawaii
735 B Sheridan St., 106D
Honolulu, HI 96814
955-4541

Dan's Dive Shop
660 Ala Moana Blvd.
Honolulu, HI 96813

Hawaii Sea Adventures
98-718 Moanalua Rd.
Pearl City, HI 96701
487-7515

Leeward Dive Center
87-066 Farrington Hwy.
Waianae, HI 96792
696-3414, 800-255-1574

Ocean Adventures
406 Kam Hwy.
Pearl City, HI 96782
487-9060

Rainbow Divers
1652 Wilikina Dr.
Wahiawa, HI 96786
622-4532

South Seas Aquatics
1050 Ala Moana Blvd.
Honolulu, HI 96814
538-3854, 800-252-MAHI

South Seas Aquatics
870 Kapahula Ave.
Honolulu, HI 96813
735-0437

Steve's Diving
1860 Ala Moana Blvd.
Honolulu, HI 96815
947-8900

Waikiki Diving Center
17344 Kalakaua Ave.
Honolulu, HI 96826
955-5151

Maui

Beach Activities Of Maui
Sheraton Maui Hotel
Lahaina, HI 96761
661-5500

Bill's Scuba Shack
36 Keala Pl.
Kihei, HI 96753
879-DIVE

Capt. Nemo's Ocean Emporium
150 Dickenson
Lahaina, HI 96761
666-5555

Central Pacific Divers
780 Front St.
Lahaina, HI 96761
661-8718, 800-551-6767

Dive Maui
Lahaina Marketplace
Lahainaluna Rd.
Lahaina, HI 96761
667-2080, 661-4363

The Dive Shop
1975 S. Kihei Rd.
Kihei, HI 96753
879-5172

Ed Robinson's
Diving Adventures
Box 616
Kihei, HI 96753
879-3584, 800-835-1273

Hawaiian Reef Divers
129 Lahainaluna Rd.
Lahaina, HI 96761
667-7647

Lahaina Divers
710 Front St.
Lahaina, HI 96761
800-657-7885

Maui Dive Shop
Azeka Pl.
Kihei, HI 96753
879-3388

Maui School Of Diving
277 Wilika Pl., Bay 21
Lahaina, HI 96761
667-5331

Mike Severns Scuba
Diving
Box 627
Kihei, HI 96753
879-6596

Ocean Enterprises
3425 Kekala Dr.
Kihei, HI 96753
879-7067

Red Sail Sports
888 Wainee St., suite 130
Lahaina, HI 96761
661-3666

Scuba Schools of Maui
1000 Limahana Pl., Suite A
Lahaina, HI 96761
661-8036

Hawaii

Aquatic Adventures
Kamuela, HI 96743
885-6068

Big Island Divers
Kona Marketplace
Kona, HI 96740
329-6068

Capt. Bob's Sea
Dreams Hawaii
Box 4886
Kona, HI 96745
329-8744

Captain Cook Cruises
74-5543 Kaiwi, Bay 11
Kona, HI 96740
329-6411

Dive Kona
Box 1780
Kona, HI 96745
800-562-3483

Dive Makai Charters
Kona Industrial Area
74-55901 Alapa
Kona, HI 96740
329-2025

Elite Dives Hawaii
67-239 B. Kahaone Lp.
Waialua, HI 96791
637-9331

Gold Coast Divers
Kona Inn Shopping Village
Kona, HI 96740
329-1328

Jack's Diving Locker
Kona Inn Shopping Village
Kona, HI 96740
329-7585

King Kamehameha Divers
75-5660 Palani Rd.
Kona, HI 96740
800-525-PADI, 329-5662

Kohala Divers
Box 44940, Kawaihae
Shopping Center
Kawaihae, HI 96743
882-7774

Kona Aggressor
Box 2097
Kona, HI 96745
329-8182

Kona Coast Divers
75-5614 Palani Rd.
Kona, HI 96740
800-KOA-DIVE, 329-8802

Kona Scuba Seafari
800-657-7704, 324-0627

Mauna Loa Diving Services
97 Haili
Hilo, HI 96720
935-3299

Nautilus Dive Center
382 Kamehameha Hwy.
Hilo, HI 96720
935-6939

Sandwich Isle Divers
76-6131 Plumeria Rd.
Kona, HI 96740
800-329-9188

Sea Paradise
78-7128 Kaleopapa Rd.
Keauhou, HI 96739
800-322-KONA, 322-2500

Kauai

Aquatics Kauai
733 Kuhio Hwy.
Kapaa, HI 96746
800-822-9422, 822-9213

Brennecke Ocean Sports
2827 Poipu Rd.
Koloa, HI 96756
742-6570

Bubbles Below Scuba
Charters
6251 Hauaala
Kapaa, HI 96746
822-3483

Dive Kauai
4-976 Kuhio Hwy., Suite 4
Kapaa, HI 96746
822-0452